RIVERSIDE COMMUNITY COLLEGE
1916

Critical Essays in Modern Literature

Other Critical Essays

William Faulkner: An Estimate of His Contribution to the Modern American Novel
by Mary Cooper Robb $1.80

The Fiction of J. D. Salinger
by Frederick L. Gwynn and
Joseph L. Blotner $1.50

Henry Miller: Expatriate
by Annette Kar Baxter $2.50

The Fiction of John O'Hara
by E. Russell Carson $1.25

James Gould Cozzens: Novelist of Intellect
by Harry John Mooney, Jr. $2.00

The Hero in Hemingway's Short Stories
by Joseph DeFalco $2.00

Entrances to Dylan Thomas' Poetry
by Ralph Maud $2.25

Joyce Cary: Comedy of Freedom
by Charles G. Hoffman $2.25

THE SHORT STORIES OF AMBROSE BIERCE

THE
SHORT STORIES
OF

Ambrose Bierce

A Study In Polarity

BY STUART C. WOODRUFF

University of Pittsburgh Press

Library of Congress Catalog Number 64-22147

To My Wife

Contents

Introduction

"TIME," Bierce once remarked to a friend, "just has a way of thrusting his mighty hand into the huge bin that we call the world and plucking from the surrounding chaff the living grains of literature." [1] Always hostile to the taste and criticism of his contemporaries, Bierce felt that time alone—the impersonal and disinterested judgment of posterity—would decide an author's reputation. In his own case, time has proved an exacting critic. From a vast amount of chaff it has culled only a few grains: *The Devil's Dictionary* and a handful of short stories which are the subject of the present study. Whatever reputation Bierce is ultimately to have (it will not be a large one) seems destined to rest on only a tiny fraction of all that he wrote during his long career. The assumption underlying this critique is that Bierce's fiction not only includes his most permanently valuable work, but also offers the clearest explanation for his limited achievement. Focusing on a few representative tales, I have tried to define Bierce's controlling conceptions, to describe his characteristic fictional devices and techniques, and to show significant parallels of theme, action, and symbolic imagery. In treating such matters, my primary concern has been to trace the causes—paradoxically the same—of Bierce's achievement and failure as a writer, and to analyze the ambivalent impulses which give his short stories their characteristic form. Although Bierce has a remarkably long bibliography for a writer so little known or read, there has been no full-length study of his fiction. There have been several biographies, innumerable articles, a few dissertations, but none have examined in any comprehensive way the kind of fictional world Bierce creates, nor have they explored the idiosyncratic relationship between his fiction and his own dilemma both as a man and as a writer.

Bierce has always had what Arnold Bennett aptly called an "underground reputation," [2] and has been the subject of more speculation, extravagant criticism, and misinformed opinion, than most American writers. One biographer gives us an idea of the range of critical response in his list of terms that have been applied to Bierce: "great, bitter, idealistic, cynical, morose, frustrated, cheerful, bad, sadistic, obscure, perverted, famous, brutal, kind, a fiend, a God, a misanthrope, a poet, a realist who wrote romances, a fine satirist and something of a charlatan." [3] Bierce is like a kaleidoscope: the individual elements remain the same but they form a different pattern for each viewer. It is no wonder that as recently as 1951, Edmund Wilson, reviewing the latest biography of Bierce, noted that "there is as yet no book on Ambrose Bierce that can really be said to come to grips with its prickly and puzzling subject," that "there are strange contradictions in Bierce that have never really been explained." [4] While it may not be possible to explain the strange contradictions in Bierce, it is possible to locate and identify them, and that has been the principal aim in this study. If Bierce has proved a protean figure, his fiction, at least, has a curiously homogeneous quality which originates in his obsessive vision. Specifically, Bierce's fiction takes its form from a series of violent oscillations between art and life, idealism and cynicism, and a richly romantic imagination and a rational awareness of life as a diminished thing. It was the pressure of the warring impulses Bierce could never manage in his own life that determined the controlling conception of his short stories. The conception itself severely restricted the range of his ideas and finally destroyed him as a serious writer. But in a handful of his war tales, it also enabled him to do what time may judge to be his finest writing.

In a letter to George Sterling, the California poet, Bierce remarked:

> How many times, and covering a period of how many years, must one's unexplainable obscurity be pointed out to constitute fame? Not knowing, I am almost disposed to consider myself the most famous of authors. I have pretty nearly ceased to be "discovered," but my notoriety as an obscurian [sic] may be said to be worldwide and apparently everlasting.[5]

If this was Bierce's curious situation near the end of his life (the letter was written in 1908), it became intensified after his disappearance in 1913. In fact, "discovering" Bierce—either the fate of the man or the stature of the writer—turned out to be something of a critical pastime, especially during the 1920's when a spate of articles appeared bearing such titles as "The Mystery of Ambrose Bierce" [6] and "Ambrose Bierce: Notorious Obscurian." [7] The only mystery in these articles is the extravagant claims they make for their subject. Rescuing a writer from supposed neglect is a risky business since the rescuer, feeling he must rationalize such a mission, often tends to overrate his man. The result is commonly a distorted image of genius suffering unjustly his sentence in literary limbo. Some of criticism's zanier estimates have produced such an image of Ambrose Bierce. Although they have little currency today, they show some of the problems involved in identifying Bierce as a writer.

In his book *On Strange Altars*, appropriately subtitled *A Book of Enthusiasms*, Paul Jordan Smith asserted:

> When young Americans leave off going to Dostoieffsky and Tchekoff for their knowledge of human nature and for some glimpse of the depths to which stricken souls may descend, . . . the greatest writer of the short story this country has yet produced may come into his own.[8]

The critic Percival Pollard, who seldom let a genius go undiscovered, was convinced that Bierce was the "greatest artist in English on our continent," "the greatest journalist, and the greatest tale-teller in America." [9] One partisan defender considered Bierce "a literary artist, one of the most delicate and finest that English literature has known. He has the savageness of Swift with the polish of Pope, and in intellect and literary feeling is the equal of both." [10] To another, not to be outdone in reckless superlatives, Bierce was "the arch prince of Literary Darkness. His light shines with clinging phosphorescence, mysterious as the night, and, like it, eternal." [11] Bierce's friend Herman Scheffauer was hopeful that some future generation would discover "the full height and measure of Bierce's greatness," although this might have to take place in Europe rather than in "our mollusc-like and Philistine civilization." [12]

Perhaps the clearest expression of this particular kind of Bierce criticism—if it may be called that—is found in one of Wilson Follett's numerous articles on Bierce and what Follett called "his brilliant obscurity." [13] Wagging a stern finger from the pages of the *Atlantic Monthly*, Follett warned:

> A nation which does not eventually salvage the treasures which a Bierce leaves accessibly buried would not deserve to breed men of genius. For a man of genius—pure literary genius—is exactly what Ambrose Bierce was. It is only a question of time, and perhaps not much time, when we shall see him emerge from the mists of his legend and appear not only as an American writer of the very first stature, but also as a world figure.[14]

Follett made his prediction in 1937; it seems no closer to being fulfilled today. Indeed, for reasons discussed in this study, none of the extravagant praise or prophecies of coming greatness that have been lavished on Bierce appear destined to stand. Bierce may well have emerged "from the mists of his legend," but he can hardly be regarded as a "writer of the very first stature," let alone a "world figure." Although Follett was hopeful about getting Bierce's "manifest destiny realized," he saw Bierce's fame largely in terms of wit and satire, the Bierce who has survived mainly in *The Devil's Dictionary;* like several critics, Follett practically ignored the tales. Calling Bierce "a man who was no story writer," Follett was sure that "if his stories as a group are deemed important it is because *he* is important; but it is not the stories that make him so." [15] How this statement is to be squared with a claim for Bierce as "pure literary genius" is unclear, but so is a good deal of the criticism represented by Follett's articles. As one anonymous writer sanely observed: "If Bierce were as great as his admirers maintain, it is almost unthinkable that his fame and fortune should never have penetrated beyond the esoteric coterie of those who have made him a cult." [16]

While not all Bierce criticism was as enthusiastic as the examples given in the preceding paragraphs, it is true that Bierce was discovered largely during the 1920's. As one of "the ghosts of underground reputations," [17] he was resurrected by a postwar generation looking for new idols, dusted off and, like Melville, praised to the skies. Critics were particularly impressed by his war stories. Disillusioned and fatalistic, filled with unsparing descriptions of death and suffering, they seemed much closer to the prevailing taste of the 1920's than to that of the 1890's. Moreover, they showed a concern with form and craftsmanship, a controlled irony, and an economy of detail that were distinctly modern. When critics cannot assign a writer a convenient niche in literary history, they frequently resort to the simple expedient of saying that he was in advance of his time. But with Bierce such a conclusion appears justified. Nothing quite like his *Tales of Soldiers and Civilians* had appeared before in American fiction, although a great deal like it has appeared since, and we have grown so accustomed to an existential world of gratuitous horror and meaningless annihilation that today Bierce seems a trifle old-fashioned. To those who had recently experienced World War I, however, and were living in its aftermath of cynicism and disillusionment, Bierce was a startling revelation. It was during this period that his reputation reached its apogee.

For a number of years after World War I, when interest in Bierce's short stories was at its height, there was no biography of him. To many readers Bierce was only a man with an unusual first name, who happened to write some powerful and depressing stories. This sketchy knowledge, combined with the strange circumstances of his disappearance, supposedly into Mexico, tended to make Bierce an intriguing man of mystery and to shroud his name in "the mists of his legend." He was said to have been a bizarre fellow who "indulged in anti-Christian orgies in cemeteries, pulled down holy crosses, exhumed corpses, loved snakes as he loathed dogs, and enjoyed meditation in graveyards, where he had once contracted asthma by sleeping on a tombstone." [18] His *Tales of Soldiers and Civilians*, reprinted in 1898 under the title *In the Midst of Life*, was generally available.[19] Boni and Liveright brought out an edition in 1918. In 1927 two editions, that of the American Library (A. and C. Boni) and that of the better-known Modern Library, were published, both with an introduction by Bierce's friend George Sterling, which did much to stimulate interest in Bierce. On the other hand, the overstuffed and expensive edition of his *Collected Works* [20]—in twelve volumes—had long been out of print, and had never been widely distributed in the first place. Because the *Collected Works* contain everything of importance that Bierce ever wrote, besides a good deal that is trivial and of no interest, it has the merit of representing Bierce both at his best and at his worst. Moreover, it shows significant relationships between the large body of his journalism and expository writing and his relatively small amount of fiction. Consequently, much of the earlier criticism of Bierce's work is based upon an imperfect knowledge of both the man and the writer.

The lack of a biography was handsomely corrected in 1929, an *annus mirabilis* for Bierce enthusiasts. In that one year, four Bierce biographies were published: Adolphe de Castro's *Portrait of Ambrose Bierce*, C. Hartley Grattan's *Bitter Bierce: A Mystery of American Letters*, Walter Neale's *Life of Ambrose Bierce*, and Carey McWilliams' *Ambrose Bierce: A Biography*. Of these, Carey McWilliams' book comes closest to being the definitive biography. McWilliams was mainly interested in dispelling or correcting the "wild and fantastic rumors" about Bierce's life; to do so he not only read through the entire body of Bierce's journalism from 1868 to 1909, but talked and corresponded with Bierce's close friends and relatives. The result is "as much a source book as it is a biography." [21] Where McWilliams is weak, however, is in the brief chapter he devotes to Bierce's fiction.[22] McWilliams simply dismisses the short stories on the assumption all were written according to an inherited formula and fail to embody any of Bierce's most deeply felt beliefs. As he puts it, "Bierce accepted a theory of aesthetics which did not accord with his own personality and his own vision." This study is intended to show, McWilliams and others notwithstanding, that Bierce's best stories not only accord fully "with his own personality," but also constitute the clearest expression of his "vision." Unfortunately, but understandably, the main point of McWilliams' biography is that Bierce "was much more interesting as a personality than he was important as a writer." [23]

Walter Neale's *Life of Ambrose Bierce* is another important book. Actually, it is not so much a biography as a collection of reminiscences by Bierce's publisher and close friend during the latter part of his life. It is especially valuable since it contains extensive summaries and quotations of Bierce's beliefs and discusses his temperament and personality in some detail. While C. Hartley Grattan's biography is reliable enough, it is not nearly as well informed as is McWilliams' book, nor does it give more than a superficial review of Bierce's fiction and journalism. Of the four biographies published in 1929, the least useful–because it is the most biased–is Adolphe de Castro's book. De Castro, whose real name was Danziger, had collaborated with Bierce on *The Monk and the Hangman's Daughter*, but the two men had a serious quarrel over the exact extent of Bierce's role in rewriting Richard Voss's *Der Mönch von Berchtesgaden.*[24] When de Castro is not justifying himself or admiring his own accomplishments, he is playing the sycophant; his book tells us more about himself than about Bierce. Since 1929 there has been only one other biography of Bierce, Paul Fatout's *Ambrose Bierce: The Devil's Lexicographer*. Fatout sees Bierce largely in terms of the impact of an unhappy childhood, the result of a stern Calvinist upbringing which Bierce renounced intellectually while permitting it to dominate his emotional life. Although this thesis has much to be said for it, the book is written, according to Edmund Wilson, "in a species of provincial journalese and characterized by a badgering and boorish tone that cheapens such distinction as Bierce possesses." [25]

What became evident as the facts were disentangled from the fancies was that in his own day Bierce was best known on the West Coast for his satirical journalism. This career spanned some forty years and made Bierce, as one friend put it, "the best hated and the best loved man in California." [26] According to George Sterling,

> Bierce, during all but the earliest years of his life in California, was our Radamanthus of letters, from whose decisions there was no appeal. With a scratch of the pen he made or broke reputations, literary or otherwise, and his pathway through time was strewn with innumerable pretenders, pierced in their vainest spots.[27]

Although the reputation Bierce established was largely a regional one, his newspaper polemics did much to spread his fame as America's most bitter cynic and misanthrope. Western readers, raised in a well-defined tradition of personal journalism, eagerly devoured his columns and looked on, fascinated, as he poured forth an endless stream of abuse on those who had offended him or who failed to meet his own standards. Some critics have found the "essential" Bierce in this journalism; to others, less impressed, he was only a writer "with a talent for turning a phrase which fluttered the parish dovecots." [28] The truth is that most of Bierce's journalism, written on topical issues and local figures, has proved highly ephemeral. Much of it lies buried in the files of obscure or long-defunct California journals and newspapers, and even the San Francisco *Examiner*, for which Bierce wrote some of his best columns, has no index for the years from 1887 to 1896 when he was a star attraction in Hearst's stable.

On the other hand, the journalism that has been preserved in the *Collected Works* has a more than parochial interest. Although the minor figures and often petty crimes on which Bierce spent so much of his energy have passed into oblivion, the larger causes of his discontent remain and help to illuminate his dilemma as a writer. His newspaper work, seldom exceptional and often merely strident in its sterile abuse, reveals a man so profoundly at odds with his age that his only means of contact with it was through ruthless cynicism and the violence of his disgust. Quite simply, Bierce hated the society that emerged from the Civil War—hated its cheap patriotism, sentimentality, and crude materialism and tastes. His assaults on all forms of mediocrity and mendacity are part of his disenchantment with America itself, in which he saw only "a great, broad blackness with two or three small points of light struggling and flickering in the universal blank of ignorance, bigotry, crudity, conceit, tobacco-chewing, ill-dressing, unmannerly manners and general barbarity." [29] Like many of this country's critics, Bierce distrusted the whole democratic experiment and scorned the notion that "in the New World the old causes would not have the old effects" or that "a republic had some inherent vitality of its own." [30] Essentially, what called forth Bierce's mockery and despair was, as Lewis Mumford remarked of Twain, "the futility of a society that denied, starved, frustrated its imaginative life, and had sacrificed every legitimate human desire for the spread of mechanical contrivances and the successes of finance." And, like Twain, Bierce translated this futility "into the futility of mankind itself." [31]

Bierce's cynicism and sense of futility, however, do more than measure the crudities of the Gilded Age, which had other critics at least as effective and perhaps more discriminating in their assaults. As certain of his essays, and particularly his letters, make evident, behind all the raillery and bitter satire lay a romantic temperament and a frustrated idealism that left Bierce stranded when he could find no way to justify them through his experience. By his own admission and the testimony of friends, Bierce had once approached life filled with extravagant expectations and youthful dreams of achievement. Specifically, this time of promise was the period covered by Bierce's war service, which Bierce always regarded as the most exciting and significant experience of his life and looked back on with an almost incredible nostalgia. It became the focal point of his existence, against which he opposed the dreary civilian aftermath, a means of defining the gulf between former youthful hopes and dreams and a present experience that mocked all sanguine assumptions about life. Bierce talked about the war, thought about it, wrote about it, all his life, and paid repeated visits to the Civil War battlefields where he had fought. Emotionally, he never left the army at all, and as his disillusionment and frustration increased, his war days became increasingly a cherished memory. As one of his characters remarks, "Youth is Gilead, in which is balm for every wound. Ah, that I might again dwell in that enchanted land!" [32] It is difficult to understand Bierce as a writer without reference to his divided sensibility and to his contradictory responses to experience. Although the conflicts in Bierce are apparent to anyone reading his journalism and correspondence, and have been remarked by Carey McWilliams and others, their relevance to his short stories has never been explored. As this study shows, however, Bierce's inability to reconcile extremes in his temperament determines the very form and texture of his imaginative world. Too many critics have regarded his fiction either as mechanically contrived or as a fictional version of his cynicism and misanthropy. While this is true of his least successful stories, it misses the significance and symbolic complexity of his war fiction, which is highly idiosyncratic.

Although Bierce always found a ready audience for his newspaper work, he had no illusions about yellow journalism or about the bitter fact that he produced far more of it than of the pure and permanent art he so revered. In his imaginative literature Bierce instinctively turned away from the prosaic constricting world dissected in his journalism. He did so either by returning to the scenes of his war experience, with all their ambiguous associations or, less successfully, by working within the tradition of terror and the supernatural. This impulse to seek out the remote or unusual, part of his romantic theory of art and the imagination, explains why Bierce never dealt in his fiction with the world of everyday experience and why his stories fall within sharply defined limits. They are circumscribed by the fact that the impulse to withdraw into a world of imagination was invariably blocked by Bierce's pervasive sense of the futility and emptiness of life itself. A recurrent pattern in Bierce's fiction is one in which the imagination is denied or frustrated by rational knowledge and empirical experience.

The qualities in Bierce's fiction which made him an exciting discovery during the 1920's had not produced the same effect in 1891 when he published *Tales of Soldiers and Civilians,* his most important collection of stories. Although the book received some favorable reviews, the response of the general reader was either indifference or distaste. In fact, Bierce could not get any of the magazines or major publishers to accept his stories, and virtually all of them appeared for the first time in the San Francisco *Examiner,* for which he had gone to work in 1887.[33] A few had been printed earlier in such papers as *The Wave* and the *Argonaut,* but a striking fact about Bierce's fiction is that almost all of it was written within a ten-year period, and much of it in his first few years with Hearst's *Examiner.* As Bierce's friend Bailey Millard remarked: "Beginning in the early 'eighties he wrote story after story, but nearly all were considered by magazine editors to be impossible for their pages; and when he sent a lot of manuscript tales to book publishers they would have none of them." [34]

Consequently, in the first edition of the *Tales,* now something of a rarity, we find the following acknowledgment: "Denied existence by the chief publishing houses of the country, this book owes itself to Mr. E. L. G. Steele, merchant, of this city. In attesting Mr.

Steele's faith in his judgment and his friend, it will serve its author's main and best ambition." With the appearance in 1893 of *Can Such Things Be?*, Bierce's career as a short story writer was just about at an end. He wrote an occasional ghost story after that time, but nothing that approached his war fiction. Stymied by the chilling metaphysic he had erected in his tales, and their indifferent reception, Bierce turned once more to his journalism and the tirade of abuse that was becoming characteristic of him.

The reaction of editors and publishers to Bierce's fiction is hardly surprising. His war stories seemed particularly offensive, with their rotting corpses and gaping wounds and their unmitigated concentration on death and suffering. About the most that could be said for them at the time was that they were a powerful indictment of war's horror, and this is how they have frequently been read. While the horror of war is real enough in these stories, that is not their ultimate concern. It is a very special kind of Civil War that is waged in Bierce's fiction, one shaped by his own conflicting responses to life. Nevertheless, his war tales were generally viewed either as antiwar tracts or as inhuman excursions into the realm of pain and death. Neither interpretation favored their acceptance by magazines which wanted "no fiction which might seriously disturb the equanimity of the family circle." [35] Bierce knew what he was up against. Of reading he remarked: "In our country it consists, as a rule, of Indiana novels, short stories in 'dialect' and humor in slang." [36] He hated the new realism, the sentimental romance, the novel itself. He refused to write a story with a happy ending, and it is even doubtful whether he could have conceived one. In one of his stories, the narrator, who has just met his fiancée at the railway station, hastens to assure us that "this is not a love story. I am no story-teller, and love as it is cannot be portrayed in a literature dominated and enthralled by the debasing tyranny which 'sentences letters' in the name of the Young Girl." [37]

There is no denying the authority of the "Young Girl" or of those who sought to serve her best interests. When she grew up, she became that formidable creature Thomas Beer calls "the Titaness," addicted to firing off letters to the editor whenever she sensed a breach of the fictional amenities.[38] Principally, these included a happy, or at least morally edifying, conclusion, total abstinence, considerable sentiment, no overt passion, and a vocabulary as tightly laced and elegantly padded as the Titaness herself. She could get *Huckleberry Finn* removed from the shelves of the Concord Library or end a play on the New York stage, and her influence upon the leading magazines and the tastes of the Gilded Age was painfully evident. "If," Beer tells us, "you were a proper editor, bred in the society of Newark or of Hartford, you did not trifle with the Titaness and for her sake you issued tales of women, by women, for women, in which one discovers the strangest things about that duel of the sexes, a deal discussed in the '90's." [39] For Bierce, she made the popular magazine "as like as one vacuum to another," [40] a view one is apt to share after glancing at the fiction that appeared in the *Cosmopolitan*, for which Bierce wrote near the end of his career. Even F. Marion Crawford, whose knowledge of popular taste made him one of America's highest-paid novelists, found that "the school-girl practically decides what we are to hear at the theater and, so far as our own language is concerned, determines to a great extent what we are to read." [41] When Bierce's tales came back from the leading magazines and publishers, it was because they seemed to flout the whole ethos of the Gilded Age. In their largest sense they expressed only the futility of his despair—the "reality" he discovered to be "the dream of a mad philosopher," "the nucleus of a vacuum." [42]

To see Bierce exclusively as a victim of circumstances, however, would be a serious misjudgment. Yet this is how he has sometimes been thought of, especially by friends and ardent admirers who made him into a figure too fine for his age, his talent hobbled by the prevailing standards of taste, his creative impulse deadened by neglect. One awed female "pupil" saw Bierce as "a sensitive, idealistic, poetic man forced by circumstance to bear silently many blows." [43] To his friend Herman Scheffauer he was "a lion in a vast squirrel-cage, a Gulliver held down by a thousand threads of public hostility, indifference and ignorance." [44] Such opinions are as misleading as others which found in Bierce only "a bitter black cynic, and a cruel, domineering old bigot." [45] All of these views are true up to a point, but their truth is only partial since they are responses to one side or another of a curiously divided personality. Insofar as Bierce was proud and sensitive in the extreme, the lack of a large or enthusiastic audience for his fiction did much to curb his efforts. But Bierce did not simply drown in a sea of sentiment. If Bierce was "held down by a thousand threads of public hostility," he was equally immobilized by his own limitations as an artist and by the nature of his vision. What remained after Bierce had rejected the literary tastes and conventions of his day was the only kind of imaginative world he could create in the first place–one utterly without joy or hope. In his journalism he appears to have seen himself in lonely rebellion against his age; in his letters, on the other hand, he is most conscious of his own inadequacies as a writer, with fine intention mocked by actual achievement. His best stories recreate the poignant contrast between his knowledge and his dream and expose the fatal conspiracy of outward circumstances and inner weakness that makes all effort useless.

Chapter I

"THE DIVINE, ETERNAL PLAN"

IN HIS JOURNALISM and satiric verse, and especially in *The Devil's Dictionary*, Bierce is primarily concerned with castigating a flawed humanity, "a world of fools and rogues, blind with superstition, tormented with envy, consumed with vanity, selfish, false, cruel, cursed with illusions—frothing mad!" [1] In his short stories, on the other hand, Bierce's characteristic theme is the inscrutable universe itself, whose mechanisms checkmate man's every attempt to assert his will or live his dreams. If the universe is not actively hostile or malevolent, as in many of his tales of the supernatural, it is at best always indifferent to human need. From birth, that "first and direst of all disasters," to death, life is but the "spiritual pickle preserving the body from decay." [2] This dismal concept of the human situation is Bierce's central imaginative impulse in his short stories, the idea that gives shape to his fictional world. Repeatedly, his protagonists become enmeshed in some fatal trap or are destroyed by uncontrollable fears. They move in ignorance toward their destiny, ground into oblivion by some spectacular ordering of events, or else unhinged by their encounter with the supernatural. To Bierce the picture was "infinitely pathetic and picturesque." [3]

Although Bierce's expository writing was largely devoted to excoriating human folly, he would occasionally hold forth upon a universe whose Maker, as Stein tells Marlow in *Lord Jim*, was a "little mad." Like many nineteenth-century pessimists, Bierce was sensitive to the implications of scientific determinism and to the operation of vast impersonal forces in nature which reduced man to the status of a puppet jerked by the strings of chance. In *The Devil's Dictionary* he defines a calamity as "a more than commonly plain and unmistakable reminder that the affairs of this life are not of our own ordering," [4] and in one of his newspaper columns he remarks: "I believe that in the word 'chance,' we have the human name of a malign and soulless intelligence bestirring himself in earthly affairs with the brute unrest of Enceladus underneath his mountain." [5] Victim of what Bierce calls in one of his tales "the pitiless perfection of the divine, eternal plan," [6] man vainly sends his prayers on high:

From Earth to Heaven in unceasing ascension flows a stream of prayer for every blessing that man desires, yet man remains unblest, the victim of his own folly and passions, the sport of fire, flood, tempest and earthquake, afflicted with famine and disease, war, poverty and crime, his world an incredible welter of evil, his life a curse and his hope a lie.[7]

As a scientific determinist, Bierce believed in evolution through natural selection, but to him it implied no march toward human perfection. Instead, he saw man caught in an eternal round of progress and disintegration. As a part of nature's principles of force and strife, man, innately selfish, engaged in an endless series of wars which destroyed the capable and strong while preserving the feeble and incompetent. Man's attempts at humanitarian and social reform, such as the rehabilitation of criminals, salvaged the very misfits and "incapables whom Nature is trying to 'weed out.'"[8] Similarly, Bierce saw a strange irony in medical science, "which is mainly concerned in reversing the beneficent operation of natural laws and saving the inefficient to perpetuate their inefficiency."[9] Scientific progress and discovery had managed to prolong man's life, but in so doing, had intensified the struggle for existence through overpopulation and increased competition. The basic paradox was that the very means by which man would save himself and improve his lot multiplied his problems instead of solving them. To Bierce, "the one goal of civilization is barbarism; to the condition whence it emerged a nation must return, and every invention, every discovery, every beneficent agency hastens the inevitable end." Consequently, "peace is more fatal than war, for all must die, and in peace more are born. The bullet forestalls the pestilence by proffering a cleaner and decenter death."[10]

Perhaps Bierce's most violent diatribe against the inhospitable universe and the clearest expression of his attitude occurs in an essay sarcastically entitled "Natura Benigna."[11] Despite the mannered and rhetorical flourishes, the violence of Bierce's assault suggests something of his own frustration and rage over a world in which "Howe'er your choice may chance to fall,/ You'll have no hand in it at all."[12] Because Bierce always insisted, as did Poe, that a storyteller must remain detached and impersonal in his narrations, such personal concern is usually disguised in his fiction. Its deliberate concealment or distortion in the direction of macabre humor has caused several of Bierce's critics to call him "inhuman" or "without pity." [13] As the following quotation from "Natura Benigna" indicates, however, Bierce's frequent claim that "nothing matters" requires careful qualification:

In all the world there is no city of refuge—no temple in which to take sanctuary, clinging to the horns of the altar—no "place apart" where, like hunted deer, we can hope to elude the baying pack of Nature's malevolences. . . . Dodge, turn and double how we can, there's no eluding them; soon or late some of them have him by the throat and his spirit returns to the God who gave it—and gave them.[14]

Particularly evident in this essay is Bierce's compulsive desire to assault what disturbs him most profoundly. The thought of that "pack of Nature's malevolences" triggers a kind of frenzied despair:

What a fine world it is, to be sure—a darling little world, "so suited to the needs of man." A globe of liquid fire, straining within a shell relatively no thicker than that of an egg—a shell constantly cracking and in momentary danger of going all to pieces! Three-fourths of this delectable field of human activity are covered with an element in which we cannot breathe, and which swallows us by myriads. . . . Of the other one-fourth more than one-half is uninhabitable by reason of climate. On the remaining one-eighth we pass a comfortless and precarious existence in disputed occupancy with countless ministers of death and pain—pass it in fighting for it, tooth and nail, a hopeless battle in which we are foredoomed to defeat. Everywhere death, terror, lamentation and the laughter that is more terrible than tears—the fury and despair of a race hanging on to life by the tips of its fingers! And the prize for which we strive, "to have and to hold"—what is it? A thing that is neither enjoyed while had, nor missed when lost. So worthless it is, so unsatisfying, so inadequate to purpose, so false to hope and at its best so brief, that for consolation and compensation we set up fantastic faiths of an aftertime in a better world from which no confirming whisper has ever reached us across the void. Heaven is a prophecy uttered by the lips of despair, but Hell is an inference from analogy.[15]

Such a chilling vision, nourished by Bierce's own experiences in the Civil War, his incisive knowledge of "how it was," provides the main creative impulse for many of his stories, especially those contained in *Tales of Soldiers and Civilians*. The war became for Bierce a controlling metaphor of the world and its ways. Always irrationally destructive, war reduced life to its lowest common denominators; the war-world he depicted made a unifying dramatic action of the hopeless struggle for existence. Its elements of surprise, confusion, and the predatory instinct constituted that blind causality which struck with devastating and unpredictable finality. The common soldier, an expendable pawn ignorant of the larger strategies and issues, was shifted about at random, fighting his enemies in treacherous forest depths or dense fog. Shells leapt out at him from nowhere, stupid or depraved officers gave disastrous orders, irrational terror overwhelmed him. Under such pressures individual will or desire became not only impossible but irrelevant, or was converted into an obsessive longing to rush wildly into certain annihilation.

The story that most clearly embodies Bierce's concept of the destructive universe is "One of the Missing." [16] Its protagonist, Jerome Searing, is a scout sent by division headquarters to reconnoiter enemy positions. "An incomparable marksman, young, hardy, intelligent and insensible to fear," Searing is presented as the ideal professional soldier. Leaving his companions behind he creeps forward stealthily and is soon "lost to view in a dense thicket of underbrush." Upon reaching the Confederate trenches he finds them empty, but moves further ahead "to assure himself beyond a doubt before going back to report upon so important a matter." He takes cover in a dilapidated plantation building which commands an excellent view of the enemy, a "half-mile away," executing an orderly withdrawal. At this point, Searing has "learned all that he could hope to know," but instead of starting back immediately for his own lines, he makes an offhand decision to send an "ounce and a quarter of lead hissing" into the midst of the retiring troops. It is a seemingly trivial act of will, unpremeditated and unmotivated.

> But it was decreed from the beginning of time that Private Searing was not to murder anybody that bright summer morning, nor was the Confederate retreat to be announced by him. For countless ages events had been so matching themselves together in that wonderful mosaic to some parts of which, dimly discernible, we give the name of history, that the acts which he had in will would have marred the harmony of the pattern.

Searing's unwitting Atropos is a Confederate artillery officer "some two miles" away from where the scout stands cocking his rifle. "Some twenty-five years previously the Power charged with the execution of the work according to the design" had caused

> the birth of a certain male child in a little village at the

foot of the Carpathian Mountains, had carefully reared it, supervised its education, directed its desires into a military channel, and in due time made it an officer of artillery. By the concurrence of an infinite number of favoring influences

the officer comes to America, joins the Confederate army, and is placed in command of a battery near Searing's observation post. "Nothing had been neglected—at every step in the progress of both these men's lives, and in the lives of their contemporaries and ancestors . . . the right thing had been done to bring about the desired result." The artillery officer makes an idle decision as seemingly inconsequential as Searing's: "Having nothing better to do while awaiting his turn to pull out and be off, [he] amused himself by sighting a field-piece obliquely to his right at what he mistook for some Federal officers on the crest of a hill, and discharged it. The shot flew high of its mark."

With the jerk of the lanyard, Searing becomes the victim of the mindless and ineluctable configurations of human destiny. With a "horrible roar," the shell "sprang at him out of the sky," smashing his hideout into "matchwood" and pinning the scout helplessly under a pile of "débris which towered above his narrow horizon." "'Jerome Searing,'" he tells himself with unnecessary emphasis, "'you are caught like a rat in a trap—in a trap, trap, trap.'" What Bierce has done in tracing the infinitely slow, infinitely complex "mosaic" of events leading up to Searing's predicament is to emphasize that the trap has existed from the beginning of time, as certain as it is inscrutable. The screaming shell and collapsed building are but the end result of that mysterious "work according to the design." Searing, "perfectly conscious of his rathood, and well assured of the trap that he was in, remembering all and nowise alarmed, again opened his eyes to reconnoitre, to note the strength of his enemy, to plan his defense."

At this point the story undergoes a significant shift in emphasis as Bierce pursues a theme closely allied to that of the destructive universe. Because of his "narrow horizon," Searing does not understand that there is no defense against the "enemy" that faces him now—his own capacity for terror. If the external ordering of events trapped the "brave" scout, it is his uncontrollable fear that finally destroys him. Like many of Bierce's stories, "One of the Missing" becomes the study of a mind coming unhinged, annihilated by its inability to cope with primitive emotions. At first Searing is relatively calm, even when he discovers that his rifle—which he mistakenly believes still cocked—points directly at his head, and that some loose boards touch the trigger. As the tension mounts the scout lapses into periods of unconsciousness and delirium. His world narrows to the "confusion of timbers and boards":

> No thoughts of home, of wife and children, of country, of glory. The whole record of memory was effaced. The world has passed away—not a vestige remained. . . . Here is immortality in time—each pain an everlasting life. The throbs tick off eternities.

Unable to place a board so as to deflect the bullet should his rifle discharge, Searing's "terror returned, augmented tenfold." Suddenly he gives up all effort to escape the trap: "a new design had shaped itself in his mind—another plan of battle." Seizing a strip of board and "closing his eyes," Searing "thrust it against the trigger with all his strength! There was no explosion; the rifle had been discharged as it dropped from his hand when the building fell. But it did its work." Later, Searing's brother, a Federal lieutenant, passes by the ruined building and notices "a dead body half buried in boards and timbers." Only twenty-two minutes have elapsed between the explosion of the artillery shell and the discovery of the body, yet Lieutenant Adrian Searing is unable to recognize the terror-twisted features of his brother: " 'Dead a week,' said the officer curtly, moving on and absently pulling out his watch as if to verify his estimate of time."

In the actions and images of "One of the Missing" we have an instructive paradigm of Bierce's fictional world of gratuitous horror and purposeless destruction. Private Searing himself is the prototype of the Biercean hero, his skill and apparent fearlessness subjected to an impossible test, his death utterly without dignity or significance, except to reveal the flawless efficiency of "the design." His lonely journey into the forest and his poignant ordeal—a frequent pattern in Bierce's war stories—constitute a kind of truncated myth in which the hero invariably fails to solve the riddle or return with the saving boon. Under the baleful gaze of an indifferent cosmos, he can only submit to his fate. The sky above Searing "appeared almost black," and even the "singing of birds, the strange metallic note of the meadow lark" makes an ominous sound "suggesting the clash of vibrant blades." In his delirium Searing falls into "pleasant memories of childhood" and dreams of the time he "entered the sombre forest . . . and with timid steps followed the faint path to Ghost Rock, standing at last with audible heart-throbs before the Dead Man's Cave and seeking to penetrate its awful mystery." His reverie is a compressed symbol of the whole pattern of his life and of man's inability to "penetrate its awful mystery." All his life Searing has been on "the faint path" that leads to "Dead Man's Cave," for the cave merges symbolically into the tiny ring of steel pointing at his head. This is what circumscribes his life and simultaneously defines man's perilous existence "in disputed occupancy with countless ministers of death and pain." As Bierce once wrote in his essay "The Ancestral Bond," "man travels, not the mental road that he would, but the one that he must—is pushed this way and that by the resultant of all the forces behind him." [17]

Bierce's fatalism is very similar to Thomas Hardy's, and both writers must necessarily rely on coincidence to enforce their particular vision. "One of the Missing," for example, is reminiscent of Hardy's poem "The Convergence of the Twain" in which the ship *Titanic* and the gigantic iceberg move relentlessly toward a collision that "jars two hemispheres." Both story and poem, moreover, point up the futility of any assertion of human will. But in a way "coincidence" is a misleading term, for Hardy and Bierce are careful to show at work an intricate pattern of causal connection, unseen by those involved but all too discernible to the detached gaze of an omniscient author.[18] As Edmund Wilson once said of Dickens's novels, the mysterious connection events have with each other becomes the moral of the tale. And in Bierce, the plot becomes the trap that snaps shut on the helpless protagonist. Virtually all of Bierce's stories, in fact, have what has been called a "snap ending"; while the term is sometimes justly used in a pejorative sense, it is important to see how Bierce's conclusions derive from his ironic point of view.[19]

In "The Mocking-bird," [20] a tale whose central features resemble those of "One of the Missing," Private Grayrock of the Federal army fires a random shot at night while on picket duty and kills his beloved brother, a Confederate soldier. The theme of divided kinsmen was a common one in stories about the Civil War, but Bierce uses it as another example of that "wondrous mosaic" destructive to the young and the brave. Grayrock's hopeless ignorance of the forces conspiring against him is symbolized by his lonely vigil in the forest: "A landscape that is all trees and undergrowth . . . lacks definition, is confused and without accentuated points upon which attention can gain a foothold." As the minutes of his watch drag by, Private Grayrock loses his sense of direction: "Lost at his post—unable to say in which direction to look for an enemy's approach . . . Private Grayrock was profoundly disquieted." When he hears "a stir of leaves and a snap of fallen twigs" he fires blindly into the dark. The next day he returns to his post to search for the man he thinks he must have killed. Like Searing, he lapses into a reverie of his happy boyhood with his brother John when they "walked in paths of light through valleys of peace, seeing new things under a new sun. And through all the golden days floated one unceasing sound—the rich, thrilling melody of a mockingbird in a cage by the cottage door." Significantly, such light-drenched scenes are now only dreams, and when Private Grayrock awakes the rays of the setting sun "projected from the trunk of each giant pine a wall of shadow traversing the golden haze to eastward until light and shade were blended in indistinguishable blue." In the "heart of the little thicket" he finds "the body of John Grayrock, dead of a gunshot wound, and still warm!" Bierce calls the strange discovery a "masterwork of civil war," brought to completion when William Grayrock kills himself out of grief and remorse.

Suicide, in fact, is committed with significant regularity in Bierce's stories, and its occurrence illuminates the very heart of his "vision of the human race, trapped and betrayed in the wilderness of the world." [21] In the war tales alone, in addition to "The Mocking-bird" and the abortive suicide of "One of the Missing," it occurs in "Killed at Resaca," "One Officer, One Man," "The Story of a Conscience," "George Thurston," and "A Tough Tussle." Bierce vigorously defended the right of "taking oneself off" if circumstances made life unbearable.[22] Among those qualifying for suicide he included people who were "threatened with permanent insanity," burdened with "disease," "addicted" to some "destructive or offensive habit," "without friends, property, employment or hope," or who had somehow "disgraced" themselves. "The time to quit," Bierce argued, "is when you have lost a big stake, your foolish hope of eventual success, your fortitude and your love of the game." [23] Since Bierce's pathetic protagonists are always losing "a big stake" or their "fortitude" to the "keeper of the table," the suicide rate in the tales is understandably high. With the paradoxical irony some modern existentialists are so fond of, Bierce regarded self-destruction as a kind of creative act, a weird moral achievement in a universe virtually drained of moral purpose and meaning. It was as if the individual could only assert his will by relinquishing it altogether in a final destructive act. Suicide became a last salute to all those dark forces conspiring against man, a Pyrrhic victory that ushered in the "good, good darkness." [24]

In "The Mocking-bird," as we have seen, suicide is prompted by grief and remorse; in "One of the Missing" Searing tries to end his suffering because of terror and overwhelming hopelessness. "The Story of a Conscience" [25] presents still another motive: guilt, coupled with an unbearable sense of disgrace. Captain Hartroy, a Federal officer, captures a Confederate spy who turns out to be one Dramer Brune, a former Union soldier who has deserted on principle to the Confederate cause. Assigned to guard Brune years before, Hartroy had fallen asleep at his post, but had been humanely wakened by Brune himself before his crime could be detected:

> "Ah, Brune, Brune, that was well done—that was great—that—"
>
> The captain's voice failed him; the tears were running down his face and sparkled upon his beard and his breast. Resuming his seat at the table, he buried his face in his arms and sobbed. All else was silence.

Here again, as in so many of his stories, Bierce enforces the ironic and tragic conjunction of events destructive of human life. The irony is not lost on Captain Hartroy. He realizes only too well that he might have saved

Brune years before by reporting his prisoner's magnanimous act, but that he failed to for fear of his own court-martial. Trapped between his obligation to have Brune shot as spy and deserter and a terrible longing to repay Brune's former generosity, Hartroy turns over his command to a fellow officer who gives the order to the firing squad. Seconds later a "single pistol shot" reveals that Captain Hartroy has "renounced the life which in conscience he could no longer keep."

By far the most important motive for Bierce's fictional suicides, however, is the inability to cope with the enemy within: one's fatal susceptibility to uncontrollable fear. To Bierce, no one was immune to its devastating effects, not even that brave and resourceful soldier, Jerome Searing. With the unpredictable suddenness of the shell that "sprang at him out of the sky," fear could reduce a man to helpless imbecility (as in many of Bierce's ghost stories), or else goad him into some spectacular act of compensatory bravery that would result in death. An inherited tendency, part of the instinctive life of the race, it was perhaps even more bitterly ironic in its lethal possibilities—and more convincing—than a whimsical ordering of external circumstance. The story "Parker Adderson, Philosopher," [26] for example, reveals the painful inadequacy of man's rational faculties when pitted against his primitive heritage. Parker Adderson, confessed spy, is seated with his captor, General Clavering, in the latter's tent. Assuming he is to be shot according to custom the following morning, Adderson dumbfounds the general by his composed attitude toward his impending death. To Clavering "Death is horrible!"; to Adderson, on the other hand, it is but "a loss of which we shall never be conscious," one that "can be borne with composure and therefore expected without apprehension." The would-be philosopher tries to explain the fear of death as an inheritance from "our savage ancestors":

> To us it is horrible because we have inherited the tendency to think it so, accounting for the notion by wild and fanciful theories of another world—as names of places give rise to legends explaining them and reasonless conduct to philosophies in justification.

At this point in Adderson's lecture, the provost marshal enters the tent and is instructed to take the spy out and shoot him immediately. Hearing that he is to die right away, Adderson suddenly goes berserk and pulls the tent down on the three of them. In the wild melee that follows, the provost marshal is stabbed to death; Clavering is mortally wounded. When order is restored we find Parker Adderson, philosopher, "cowered upon the ground" uttering "unintelligible remonstrances." As he is led away "begging incoherently for his life," General Clavering, the man who had thought death "horrible," dies serenely, "with a smile of ineffable sweetness" upon his face.

The instinctive hereditary fear that unravels Parker Adderson as a rational human being leads directly to the protagonist's suicide in "One Officer, One Man," and in "George Thurston,"[27] In the former tale we find Captain Graffenreid facing his first experience under fire after an irksome tour of duty at his state capitol. Aware that his battle-hardened companions assume he has been "forced unwillingly into the field,"

Graffenreid looks forward buoyantly to proving himself in combat:

He was in a state of mental exaltation and scarcely could endure the enemy's tardiness in advancing to the attack. . . . How his heart leaped in his breast as the bugle sounded the stirring notes of "assembly"! With what a light tread, scarcely conscious of the earth beneath his feet, he strode forward at the head of his company, and how exultingly he noted the tactical dispositions which placed his regiment in the front line! And if perchance some memory came to him of a pair of dark eyes that might take on a tenderer light in reading the account of that day's doings, who shall blame him for the unmartial thought or count it a debasement of soldierly ardor?

In a style that simultaneously mocks the language of romantic adventure tales and Graffenreid's naïve concept of his heroic possibilities, Bierce sets up his central contrast between, on the one hand, the individual's illusion of freedom and self-determination and, on the other, some combination of inherent frailty and external circumstance that inevitably defeats the protagonist.[28] A similar contrast is established in "One of the Missing," through the opening descriptions of Searing's bravery and professional competence, or in Private Grayrock's sentimental reverie of his youthful days in "the paths of light" and the "valleys of peace." Many of Bierce's most successful stories are stories of initiation in which the opportunity to profit by hard-won understanding is terminated by violent death, or in which the insight itself makes life unbearable. The movement is typically from some illusion of life's sunny promise to an annihilating forest experience. For example, several of Bierce's tales begin with a reference to sunshine: "One sunny afternoon in the autumn of the year 1861" ("A Horseman in the Sky"); "The time, a pleasant Sunday afternoon in the early autumn of 1861. The place a forest's heart" ("The Mocking-bird"); "One sunny autumn afternoon" ("Chickamauga"). In all of these stories the setting belies the true state of affairs and sets up a cruel contrast between appearance and reality, a fatal imbalance between desire and achievement. While Bierce's plots have received considerable attention, largely from the standpoint of their artificiality or mechanical ingenuity, his symbolic use of setting has gone virtually unnoticed. One reason for the superiority of the war stories over his supernatural tales, however, is that in the former Bierce's settings and dramatic actions often function as integrated metaphors for the process of psychological collapse.

Graffenreid's initiation into the harsh realities of life begins when the enemy fires an artillery barrage "from the forest a half-mile in front." Cowering from a shell which explodes harmlessly to his left, he hears "a low, mocking laugh" from his first lieutenant.

> He had not known that the flight of a projectile was a phenomenon of so appalling character. His conception of war had already undergone a profound change, and he was conscious that his new feeling was manifesting itself in visible perturbation.

Forced to take cover beside a dead soldier, Graffenreid gets an instructive worm's-eye view of the face of death: "It looked yellow already, and was repulsive. Nothing suggested the glory of a soldier's death nor mitigated the loathsomeness of the incident." During a momentary lull in the action "had come introspection. He sought rather to analyze his feelings than distinguish himself by courage and devotion. The result was profoundly disappointing. He covered his face with his hands and groaned aloud." When the order is given to attack, Graffenreid is paralyzed with fear. He stares transfixed at "the sinister silence of the forest in front." Seconds later a sergeant behind the terrified officer sees a strange sight: "a sudden reaching forward of the hands and their energetic withdrawal, throwing the elbows out, as in pulling an oar." From between the officer's shoulders springs "a bright point of metal which prolonged itself outward, nearly a half-arm's length—a blade!"

The protagonist in "George Thurston," instead of becoming suddenly aware of his cowardice, knows it all along and tries to subdue it by recklessly exposing himself to danger. As the stammering quartermaster explains the matter at mess one day, "It's h-is w-ay of m-m-mastering a c-c-consti-t-tu-tional t-tendency to r-un aw-ay." Inflexible and aloof, Thurston fights his private war by walking into the hottest battles with arms folded and head erect. Although he is wounded, he leads an apparently charmed life. Back in camp one day, he joins a group of men amusing themselves on a swing some fifty feet high. Pumping himself to dizzying heights, heedless of the warnings from below, Thurston soon drives his swing past the level of its anchorage. Suddenly the rope goes slack and Thurston, catapulted out beyond its arc, lands with a sickening impact. When they reach his mangled body they find the arms "folded tightly across the breast." Of death itself the shaken narrator remarks: "We did not know that he had so ghastly resources, possibilities of terror so dismal." George Thurston, the "man in the sky," a speck "sharply outlined against the blue," becomes a symbol of man's pitiful existence in an alien world.

The fate that overtakes such characters as Jerome Searing, William Grayrock, and George Thurston, originates in what Bierce conceived of as the "pitiless perfection of the divine, eternal plan." Whether this fate manifests itself as some arbitrary pattern of external circumstance or as an inner "constitutional tendency" makes no difference. The result is the same: the annihilation of the protagonist or of his private dream. Sometimes death is preceded by a stupefying sense of disillusionment or horror; sometimes it comes so swiftly there is no time for reflection. In many of the war stories, Bierce creates a bitter contrast between the main character's hopes or youthful dreams and the harsh reality that reduces him to a meaningless cipher. Focusing on single moments of intense crisis and awareness, Bierce shows his characters being hounded into a corner where their affliction becomes "an acclimatizing process preparing the soul for another and bitter world."[29] Their brief life in present time is "a little plot of light" where "we enter, clasp a hand or two, and go our several ways back into the darkness."[30] Death ends their dreams of that "imaginary period known as the Future," the "realm of song" where "Hope flies with a free wing, beckoning to temples of success and bowers of ease."[31] To Bierce, the ultimate horror of the "eternal plan" was that man could learn nothing from his ordeal except the lesson of his own futility and purposelessness. Perhaps this was the "awful mystery" that Jerome Searing, in his delirium, tried to "penetrate" as he stood before "Dead Man's Cave." Like Searing, Bierce found existence to be "A transient, horrible, fantastic dream,/Wherein is nothing yet all things do seem." [32]

It is this nightmarish quality of experience, in which reality grotesquely mocks appearance, that Bierce achieves in one of his finest stories.[33] "What an allegory is 'Chickamauga' . . . !" wrote an anonymous reviewer in 1898.[34] And that is what the story is—a moral fable which embodies in the child's horrible experience the dislocation of man's dream of subduing his world. In a sense, what Bierce has done in "Chickamauga" is to subvert the Wordsworthian claim that the child is father to the man by showing it true in a way that turns hope to horror and despair. The story's fundamental insight is that through an inherited "lust for war" man carries within him the seeds of his own destruction. He can no more eliminate his predatory instinct than he can his susceptibility to paralyzing fear, and he transmits both to his offspring. His flawed humanity manifests itself as an enervating struggle between cowardice and aggression, the need to attack and wound coupled with the need to retreat and run away. Both impulses Bierce saw as natural "predilections," a term he defines in *The Devil's Dictionary* as "the preparatory stage of disillusion." [35]

The nameless child protagonist of "Chickamauga" is a deaf-mute, oblivious to the sounds of battle raging near his home. Entering a forest "one sunny autumn afternoon," the boy experiences an exhilarating "sense of freedom from control," a yen for adventure, "for this child's spirit, in bodies of its ancestors, had for thousands of years been trained to memorable feats of discovery and conquest." His father, we are told at the beginning of the story, "had been a soldier" and "the warrior-fire survived; once kindled, it is never extinguished." With his wooden sword brandished bravely, "as became the son of an heroic race," the child delights in various "postures of aggression and defense." He subdues his invisible enemies with incredible ease and pursues them across a shallow brook where he "fell again upon the rear-guard of his imaginary foe, putting all to the sword." The most noticeable aspect of the child's military pantomime is its complete naturalness—his instinctive delight in the *idea* of power and aggression. In *The Devil's Dictionary*, Bierce defines "behavior" as "conduct, as determined, not by principle, but by breeding." [36]

This same idea of biological determinism—part of the trap man is born into—he discusses at some length in his essay "The Ancestral Bond":

> My own small study in this amazing field [heredity] convinces me that a man is the sum of his ancestors; that his character, moral and intellectual, is determined before his birth. His environment with all its varied suasions, its agencies of good and evil; breeding, training, interest, experience and the rest of it—have less to do with the matter and cannot annul the sentence passed upon him at conception, compelling him to be what he is.[37]

Bierce saw heredity as simply another instrument of the inscrutable plan, part of the general "sentence" imposed upon mankind by a whimsical destiny. If

Bierce's characters lack psychological complexity, a partial explanation is that Bierce was more concerned with certain generic human traits than with specific or idiosyncratic qualities.

As the deaf-mute starts back home he is suddenly frightened by a rabbit sitting upright in his path. In an ironic reversal somewhat too heavily insisted upon, the "son of an heroic race" flees in panic, "calling with inarticulate cries for his mother, weeping, stumbling, his tender skin cruelly torn by brambles, his little heart beating hard with terror—breathless, blind with tears—lost in the forest!" Exhausted, he sobs himself to sleep; when he awakes, it is dusk. "A thin, ghostly mist rose along the water. It frightened and repelled him; instead of recrossing, in the direction whence he had come, he turned his back upon it, and went forward toward the dark inclosing wood." At this point his initiation into a world of surrealistic horror begins, an initiation climaxed when his "retreat" brings him back to his fire-gutted home and the mangled corpse of his mother. While the child slept, a furious battle had taken place. Soldiers "had penetrated the forest in thousands. Their successive battalions, breaking into swarms and re-forming in lines, had passed the child on every side—had almost trodden on him as he slept." Except to grasp "his little wooden sword with perhaps a tighter clutch in unconscious sympathy with his martial environment," the deaf-mute sleeps soundly until the battle is over.

Because the child is both ignorant and deaf, what we now witness through his eyes is a crazy, gruesome dumb show, horrible in its silent intensity. As far as the eye can see, the forest is filled with wounded soldiers creeping and dragging themselves toward the rear: "They came by dozens and by hundreds; as far on either hand as one could see in the deepening gloom they extended and the black wood behind them appeared to be inexhaustible. The very ground seemed in motion toward the creek." To enforce the horror of the scene, Bierce shows the child's grotesquely inappropriate responses to the wounded men. Totally unaware of their significance, the boy moves among them freely "peering into their faces with childish curiosity." The first man he notices "he took to be some large animal—a dog, a pig—he could not name it; perhaps it was a bear." With their white twisted faces streaked with blood and grime and their "grotesque attitudes and movements" they remind the child "of the painted clown whom he had seen last summer in the circus. . . ." "To him it was a merry spectacle." Having ridden his father's slaves as they crept on all fours "for his amusement," the child now leaps on the back of one of the crawling men:

> The man sank upon his breast, recovered, flung the small boy fiercely to the ground as an unbroken colt might have done, and then turned upon him a face that lacked a lower jaw—from the upper teeth to the throat was a great red gap fringed with hanging shreds of flesh and splinters of bone. The unnatural prominence of nose, the absence of chin, the fierce eyes, gave this man the appearance of a great bird of prey crimsoned in throat and breast by the blood of its quarry.

Recovering from his momentary fright, the child places himself at the head of the "hideous pantomime" and, "his wooden sword still in hand," leads his "swarm of great black beetles" toward an eerie red glow in the distance. When he reaches "the blazing ruin of a dwelling," he fails at first to recognize his own home and, excited by the fire, dances "with glee in imitation of the wavering flames." Then, with the child's sudden crushing insight, life becomes for him what Bierce called the "transient, horrible, fantastic dream." The outbuildings assume "an oddly familiar appearance, as if he had dreamed of them." Then "the entire plantation, with its inclosing forest, seemed to turn as if upon a pivot. His little world swung half around; the points of the compass were reversed." Waking from his previous fantasies, he finds that the nightmare has become reality, and he is "stupefied by the power of the revelation." [38] His final discovery is the mutilated body of his mother. At the end he stands "motionless, with quivering lips, looking down upon the wreck."

In responding to the child's ordeal and his poignant lack of awareness until the last devastating moment, readers are apt to miss the larger meaning implicit in "Chickamauga." Bierce is not finally concerned with the pathos of the child himself or even with the horrors of war, ironically revealed, although both these meanings exist. His main insight is that the child carries in him the same instinctive forces and impulses which send the wounded soldiers crawling crazily through the forest and which demolish his world. In the opening paragraphs Bierce underscores the child's innocent delight in games of war and especially the instinctive origin of this "warrior-fire" which, "once kindled," is "never extinguished." The boy's attack upon imaginary foes, followed by his flight from the rabbit, is an ironic parallel to the soldiers' grim retreat. Of their footprints near the creek Bierce remarks: "An observer of better experience in the use of his eyes would have noticed that these footprints pointed in both directions; the ground had been twice passed over—in advance and in retreat." The child's apparently trivial experience at the beginning of the story takes on a terrible significance as Bierce establishes its essential identity with an adult world of impossible suffering in which the soldiers "were men, yet crept like babes."

With his buoyant aggressiveness, coupled with a susceptibility to pain and terror, the child is indeed father to the man, an appropriate figure to lead the band of pitiful casualties. What springs shut on him in the fitful glare of "the inclosing forest" is the trap of his own flawed humanity. To the child the soldiers at first look like animals—pigs, dogs, bears; the man he tries to ride is "a great bird"; the movement of the wounded resembles "a swarm of great black beetles." Such imagery suggests Bierce's sense of man's inherent bestiality and the dehumanization it causes. But the child also exhibits the same bestial impulse in mounting the wounded soldier as he had done with his father's slaves. When he finds his mother's body he emits "a series of inarticulate and indescribable cries—something between the chattering of an ape and the gobbling of a turkey—a startling, soulless, unholy sound, the language of a devil." Both the boy and the soldiers have their ordeal by fire, their forest initiation; what they experience reduces them to something subhuman: "a pig," "an ape," "a devil."

The horror of "Chickamauga" is the horror of Bierce's own despairing fatalism which saw man as victim either of his own inadequacies or of some destructive configuration of circumstance. Whatever the forces against him, man is viewed as incapable of controlling his own destiny or even of alleviating his suffering except by death. With this knowledge Bierce's characters discover that the nightmare has become the true reality and that their once vivid sensations of freedom and conquest have become the empty mocking dream. It is then that they find their "little world swung half around," the "points of the compass" "reversed." When this occurs the story can go no further. Bierce has had his final say, for in showing the assumed normative values to be either false or ineffectual, he can offer nothing in their place except some stoical act of submission to the inevitable. In fact, under the conditions of Bierce's fictional world, the ultimate meaning of one's existence is its meaninglessness. At this point, the only thing to do is to fold one's arms across one's breast and, like George Thurston, leap into space. "Pain is cruel, death is merciful," Bierce once wrote in defense of euthanasia. "Prolongation of a mortal agony is hardly less barbarous than its infliction. Who when sane in mind and body would not choose to guard himself against a futile suffering by an assurance of accelerated release?" [39]

Writing to a young female admirer in 1901, Bierce expressed the hope that she was "well and happy—as happy as it is consonant with the plans of God's universe for any of his helpless creatures to be—or believe themselves to be." [40] This sense of man's helplessness, of the terrible inevitability of his fate, is the most persistent theme running through Bierce's stories, especially those dealing with war. For Bierce, war was the ideal metaphor to define the human predicament, not simply because he had known war intimately, but because it was the clearest demonstration of how the instinctive and the accidental combined to thwart human endeavor. But war's most important function was to represent what Bierce regarded as the central fact of existence: one's physical annihilation. Believing that the "mind or spirit or soul of man was the product of his physical being, the result of chemical combinations," [41] Bierce looked upon death as the "awful mystery," awful because of its irreducible finality, its negation of all of man's hopes and creative impulses. As his friend David Jordan wrote: "Whether glory or conquest or commercial greed be war's purpose the ultimate result of war is death. Its essential feature is the slaughter of the young, the brave, the ambitious, the hopeful." [42] Bierce's war stories are fables of life's essential movement toward disillusion, defeat, and death. They concentrate and accelerate the inexorable process of disintegration. Thus the demolished building in "One of the Missing" becomes Searing's "sole universe" as his "throbs tick off eternities," and the child in "Chickamauga" has "his little world swung half around" in a matter of hours.

For reasons that will be discussed in a subsequent chapter on Bierce's severe limitations as an artist, his stories always fall short of tragedy. Nevertheless, in the best of them, to be found among the tales of soldiers, there is a genuine pathos that arises from Bierce's intense awareness of a suffering humanity. Nowhere is this pathos more movingly achieved than in a story called "The Coup de Grâce." [43] Although Sergeant Halcrow is not a criminal, he is "condemned" to the sentence of death that hangs over all, and the *coup de grâce*, the merciful blow that ends his agony, is delivered not by the executioner, but by his closest friend, Captain Madwell. For different reasons, both men are hopelessly trapped, and their ordeal in the "haunted forest" epitomizes the plight of all whom, sooner or later, Bierce saw undone by the eternal plan. In Bierce's most convincing stories we see little of that intemperate and sometimes hysterical assault on human folly that characterizes his expository writing; that is, his main characters are seldom the object of the narrator's scorn or abuse. Bierce is conscious of unmerited suffering and his despair is consequently centered not so much on man as on the destructive nature of his experience. This focus enabled him to manage tone more successfully in his war tales than in his other writings, and while it did not prevent his showing the human condition to be meaningless, it kept it from becoming merely absurd.

Significantly, "The Coup de Grâce" begins with the battle already concluded. Not war, but war's aftermath is its proper concern—war's effect in human terms.

All was now over; it remained only to succor the wounded and bury the dead—to "tidy up a bit," as the humorist of a burial squad put it. A good deal of "tidying up" was required. As far as one could see through the forests, among the splintered trees, lay wrecks of men and horses.

Bierce has sometimes been accused of being heartless or even cynically amused in his war stories, but this is not true.[44] The charge probably stems from a failure to assess properly Bierce's characteristic tone as narrator. In the passage quoted above, the tone somewhat resembles that of Hemingway. For example, there is the ominous ambiguity of "all was now over," and the macabre understatement of the hardened soldier on the burial squad, which the narrator immediately picks up. Then, in the slow cadences of the last sentence, suggesting an endless expanse of waste and slaughter, we see the necessity for the narrator's controlled, matter-of-fact voice; it is a means of objectifying his own sense of horror. Bierce is not always so successful in the management of tone, but his own attitudes in the war stories can usually be detected beneath a masking voice of ironic and tight-lipped understatement.

While the burial party goes about its task, Captain Madwell, "a daring and intelligent officer, an honorable man," leans wearily against a tree. Sergeant Halcrow, Madwell's best friend, has served in the captain's outfit, but is missing in action following a fierce battle that morning. The two men had "grown up together from childhood" and have always been inseparable. In fact, Halcrow had enlisted in his friend's company—"a habit of the heart is not easily broken off." Their commanding officer is the sergeant's brother, Major Creede Halcrow, "a cynical, saturnine man" who has developed a violent hatred of Madwell. Just that morning the major had cast a sneering aspersion on Madwell's bravery, to which the captain replied, "I have long held the opinion that it would be better if you were dead." When the burial party leaves, Captain Madwell walks "straight away into the forest toward the red west, its light staining his face like blood." In the gathering dusk he carefully goes over the ground of the recent battle until he discovers the body of his friend: "He looked at it narrowly. It seemed to stir. He stooped and laid his hand upon its face. It screamed."

From this moment until the revelation of the last sentence, the story focuses unsparingly on the single experience of Halcrow's impossible agony and the captain's tormented compassion. The nature of the sergeant's wound puzzles Madwell:

> His leather belt was parted and had apparently been dragged from beneath him as he lay. There had been no great effusion of blood. The only visible wound was a wide, ragged opening in the abdomen. It was defiled with earth and dead leaves. Protruding from it was a loop of small intestine. In all his experience Captain Madwell had not seen a wound like this.

Rising and looking around, the captain sees the sickening explanation:

> Fifty yards away, on the crest of a low, thinly wooded hill, he saw several dark objects moving about among the fallen men—a herd of swine. One stood with its back to him, its shoulders sharply elevated. Its forefeet were upon a human body, its head was depressed and invisible. The bristly ridge of its chine showed black against the red west.

What Madwell stares at is the obscenity of death itself,

an obscenity which has "defiled" the body of Sergeant Halcrow and defined his humanity as an unbearable sensitivity to pain and suffering. Victim of "monstrous mutilations" Halcrow's "giant agony" has reduced him to an "it," "the thing which had been" Madwell's friend. All that remains is the mute appeal in the eyes "imploring everything, all, the whole non-ego, for the boon of oblivion."

There is no missing Halcrow's significance. He is "this writhing fragment of humanity, this type and example of acute sensation, this handiwork of man and beast." Above all, he is "this humble, unheroic Prometheus," who has been granted the suffering without the glory. His vitals are torn, not by the noble bird of prey, but by a herd of roving swine; he is "incarnate suffering." Despite its painful explicitness, "The Coup de Grâce" manages to avoid both sensationalism and sadism. What preserves it from becoming either—the only thing—is the compassion of Captain Madwell, the reality of his concern which enables him to administer the *coup de grâce:*

> Captain Madwell spoke the name of his friend. He repeated it over and over without effect until emotion choked his utterance. His tears plashed upon the livid face beneath his own and blinded himself. He saw nothing but a blurred and moving object. . . . He turned away, struck his hand upon his forehead, and strode from the spot.

Stumbling over a maimed horse which "lifted its head sidewise and neighed piteously," Captain Madwell shoots the animal between the eyes: "The tense muscles of its lips, which had uncovered the teeth in a horrible grin, relaxed; the sharp, clean-cut profile took on a look of profound peace and rest."

When Madwell finally summons nerve to end his friend's torment, he discovers to his horror that he has used his last cartridge on the horse. Drawing his sword and sighting along its edge "as if to test his nerves," he sees no "tremor of the blade" in the "ray of bleak skylight." Without averting his eyes, he leans his weight upon the hilt and sends the blade through Halcrow's heart and into the ground beneath.

At that moment three men stepped silently forward from behind the clump of young trees which had concealed their approach. Two were hospital attendants and carried a stretcher.

The third was Major Creede Halcrow.

The ending is not simply one more gratuitous horror, applied for its shock value. It originates in Bierce's conception of the very nature of things. The fate that has silently stalked Captain Madwell in the "haunted forest" has done more than mock his merciful act; it has made it the occasion for his own destruction. Always in the end, to use Bierce's favorite phrase, "nothing matters." The trap springs shut.

The image of man which Bierce's war stories reflect is that of a "humble, unheroic Prometheus," incapable of dominating circumstance or of converting his will into permanently significant action. Faced with forces within and without that invariably overpower him, only his capacity for suffering gives him a kind of pathetic significance. He is, as someone has said of Hemingway's protagonists, the hero to whom things happen. In an essay that illuminates Bierce's attitude, not only in "The Coup de Grâce" but in virtually all of his serious fiction, he wrote:

> It is urged that not knowing the purposes of the Creator in creating and giving us life, we should endure . . . whatever ills befall, lest by death we ignorantly frustrate the divine plan. Merely pausing to remark that the plan of an omnipotent Deity is not easily frustrated, I should like to point out that in this very ignorance of the purpose of existence lies a justification of putting an end to it. I did not ask for existence; it was thrust upon me without my assent. As He who gave it has permitted it to become an affliction to me, and has not apprised me of its advantages to others or to Himself, I am not bound to assume that it has any such advantages.[45]

Although an avowed agnostic, Bierce was no atheist nor, for that matter, was he ever able to shake himself free of his early Calvinist upbringing, despite his frequent jibes at all dogmatic theology. He could readily imagine an "omnipotent Deity" controlling human destiny from motives impossible to fathom, but the idea of a God lovingly concerned with the affairs of mankind was inconceivable.

> Fear not in any tongue to call
> Upon the Lord—He's skilled in all.
> But if He answereth my plea
> He speaketh one unknown to me.[46]

And then there was the ominous possibility that

> perhaps God *is* "a deceiver"; who knows that he is not? Assumption of the existence of a God is one thing; assumption of the existence of a God who is honorable and candid according to our conception of honor and candor is another.[47]

Maintaining that "a mind congenitally gifted with the

power of logic and accessible to its light and leading does not take to religion," he viewed all religions as "conclusions for which the facts of nature supply no major premises." [48]

The congealing sense of doom that permeates Bierce's war stories suggests a Calvinism from which all sense of grace or benevolent purpose has been removed. As one critic has put it:

> Bierce had rejected the God of his New England ancestors and his Puritan upbringing, but the code that he retained implied a metaphysic almost identical to the Calvinism that he denied. A harshly personal God was replaced by a harshly impersonal Fate. Every man's slightest action was preordained, and his duty was to submit to the mysterious workings of the supernatural.[49]

One important effect of this rigid fatalism is to minimize or ignore the question of man as moral agent in favor of portraying the effects of a deterministic universe. This is not to say that Bierce was indifferent to moral values—the whole body of his journalism and satire shows how accountable he held man. But in the short stories his characters have no inner moral life in any decisive sense. What they do have is a kind of rudimentary psychology which reacts according to the stimulus they receive and their "constitutional tendency." Bierce's characters are really human types—types of susceptibility—rather than fully drawn individuals. They may have a history, but they lack an identity apart from the circumstances they are exposed to.

Since these circumstances are invariably destructive in one way or another, the story ends when the maximum pressure has been brought to bear on the protagonist. If he does not actually die, at the very least his private world collapses and death would even seem preferable—the "boon of oblivion" that Madwell accords his friend. He is a "humble, unheroic Prometheus" because his suffering serves no discernible purpose, and because his fate is not something consciously risked in defiance of the gods. Fate, like Major Halcrow concealed in the "haunted forest," simply comes upon him unaware. If the protagonist commits suicide, it is either because he realizes he is inextricably caught or because, like George Thurston, he has long recognized his fate as some inherent compulsion which makes life unbearable. In any event Bierce's characters are never responsible for what happens to them. Often, like Captain Madwell or Jerome Searing, they are good, brave men or, like the child in "Chickamauga," merely ignorant and naïve. Essentially passive, sometimes literally immobilized like Prometheus in his chains, they have an interior life of acute sensation. Because we can know them only through their feelings, which are usually very unpleasant or painful, we can only respond to them with pity. We do not really know *them;* we know their suffering.

Because it was the reality of their suffering and frustration that Bierce responded to, his war figures make a serious claim upon our attention. Only in the war stories does Bierce achieve the sense of genuine concern for human frailty endlessly cheated and baffled by life. His characters are credible even when their dilemmas are not, because he believed in the agony of their ordeal, even if he believed in little else.

Chapter II

WAR AS THE DRAMA OF LOST ILLUSIONS

THERE IS LITTLE DOUBT that the Civil War was the pivotal experience of Bierce's life, and no one was more aware of its centrality than Bierce himself. Throughout a career that covered some forty years, he wrote about the war regularly, talked about its prominent leaders and strategies, and several times visited the battlefields where he had fought.[1] Just before his disappearance in 1913, when he was over seventy, he made a lonely pilgrimage that took him over the scenes of virtually every engagement he had been in. Walking as much as fifteen miles a day under a hot October sun, Bierce spent three weeks visiting such places as Missionary Ridge, Chickamauga, Stone River, Franklin, and Shiloh, following the battlefield markers and noting carefully the positions of his own outfit.[2] Bierce's motives in making such a journey are obscure; certainly his war days were always so vivid in his mind that he hardly needed the actual scenes to recall them, and one does not do the amount of walking Bierce did at seventy merely to satisfy an historical interest in military engagements. There was something compulsive about the undertaking, as if Bierce were trying to retrace the circumstances of his life—to get back to some seminal point that could define all that had happened to him.

Bierce came very close to making the army a career; had it not been for the fact that he found only a second lieutenant's commission waiting for him in San Francisco instead of the hoped-for captaincy, he no doubt would have stayed in the army.[3] Nevertheless, throughout his life Bierce maintained a kind of habitual military posture which, if not directly derived from his war service, at least revealed a mind congenial to an authoritarian world of rules, precision, and strict discipline. It showed up in every facet of his life—in his erect carriage and passion for personal neatness, in his physical courage, in the authoritarian way in which he addressed even his closest friends. Above all, it manifested itself in his journalism as an instinctive impulse to assault anything and everything that gave offense, to use language as a weapon to destroy a civilian world of fools and rogues. One British magazine carried a cartoon depicting Bierce, eyes flashing fire, drawing a pen from a scabbard; that is precisely the use to which he put his pen—to wound, if not to kill. Bierce's military ways even colored his vocabulary and affected his style, whose best qualities, as Edmund Wilson has pointed out, are "military—concision, severe order, unequivocal clearness." [4]

But if Bierce was military in his bearing and habits, often offensively so, he was not warlike. This distinction Bierce made in an essay entitled "Warlike America," in which he assailed McKinley's claims that America had "never gone to war for conquest, for exploitation or for territory, but always for liberty and humanity." A "military" people, Bierce remarked, studies the "arts and sciences of war," a "warlike" people is simply "fond of war." What Bierce resented was the hypocrisy of the President's statement, which Bierce disputed by saying that "the slightest acquaintance with history shows that powerful republics are the most warlike and unscrupulous of nations." [5] Bierce was always a keen and well-informed student of war's "arts and sciences," but he had no illusions about its motives and effects, and hated the noisy jingoism so prevalent at the end of the century. In fact, he was not even sure where his sympathies had been in the Civil War: "I know what uniform I wore–/ O, that I knew which side I fought for!" [6] And when he felt especially bitter, he used to say he had "hired out as an assassin" for his country.

As his final inspection of the old battle scenes suggests, Bierce's most deeply felt attitudes toward the Civil War had relatively little to do with a delight in military tactics, or even with the satisfaction he derived from having proved himself a brave and competent officer during four years of heavy fighting. Despite the hardships and horrors, Bierce looked upon his service years as the highest and brightest of his life, a period of thrilling adventure that made the civilian aftermath a dreary anticlimax. Once he wrote an article urging that an overgrown, forgotten Confederate burial ground in West Virginia be converted to a properly maintained cemetery. Of the neglected dead he observed:

> They were honest and courageous foemen, having little in common with the political madmen who persuaded them to their doom and the literary bearers of false witness in the aftertime. They did not live through the period of

honorable strife into the period of vilification—did not pass from the iron age to the brazen—from the era of the sword to that of the tongue and pen. . . . Their valor was not the fury of the noncombatant; they have no voice in the thunder of the civilians and the shouting. Not by them are impaired the dignity and infinite pathos of the Lost Cause.[7]

If the war was an iron age, Bierce wrote about it as if it had been a golden one, and nowhere more extravagantly or nostalgically than in the essays in the *Collected Works* grouped under the heading "Bits of Autobiography." As the title indicates, these essays contain only fragmentary biographical information. Nevertheless, they are valuable for understanding Bierce as a writer, since they reveal conflicting aspects of his perception which ultimately made fiction impossible for him. The essays are particularly useful as evidence of a strain of emotional fervor and romantic idealism which Bierce found increasingly untenable in the face of certain indigestible facts of his experience. Viewed in this light, the war stories show his obsessive concern with the disparity between assumptions about life and life's actual conditions. An essentially destructive universe mocks every human effort and desire, every illusion about life's possibilities. The war would seem to have been that moment in Bierce's life which first drove home the fatal split between what one hopes for from life and what one gets. But even more important, it was the time of youth's resiliency, the time he defined as the "Period of Possibility," "the true Saturnian Reign, the Golden Age on earth again."[8]

What binds together the essays in "Bits of Autobiography" is not so much their subject matter as the emotionally heightened and occasionally rhapsodic style in which they are written. Carey McWilliams says of them:

He never related a mean experience about his life; he selected only the "grand" episodes and wrote of them after the manner of an elderly gentleman entertaining a circle of excited ladies. . . . His "memoirs" are told in the manner of a professional *raconteur*, and were selected solely for their dramatic possibilities as stories and for the romantic halo which they cast about his own life. He bows, in these memoirs, more than once to the galleries.[9]

As a biographer, McWilliams is understandably disappointed to find "Bits of Autobiography" so "misleading," but the very liberties Bierce takes in the interest of idealizing experience tell us a good deal. Actually, what Bierce says or does not say is not so important as his tone. What concerns us are the emotional attitudes he reveals.

"What I Saw of Shiloh," the longest and most revealing of the essays, ends with this passage:

O days when all the world was beautiful and strange; when unfamiliar constellations burned in the Southern midnights, and the mocking-bird poured out his heart in the moon-gilded magnolia; when there was something new under a new sun; will your fine, far memories ever cease to lay contrasting pictures athwart the harsher features of this later world, accentuating the ugliness of the longer and tamer life? Is it not strange that the phantoms of a blood-stained period have so airy a grace and look with so tender eyes?—that I recall with difficulty the danger and death and horrors of the time, and without effort all that was gracious and picturesque? Ah, Youth, there is no such wizard as thou! Give me but one touch of thine artist hand upon the dull canvas of the Present; gild for but one moment the drear and somber scenes of to-day, and I will willingly surrender an other life than the one that I should have thrown away at Shiloh.[10]

Readers who know Bierce only as the detached, self-contained narrator of *Tales of Soldiers and Civilians* might well find such purple prose somewhat surprising, or assume that the essay was written in Bierce's "anecdotage." The fact is, however, that "What I Saw of Shiloh" was begun while Bierce was in England in the 1870's and was published in the San Francisco *Wasp* in December of 1881.[11] This was several years before the stories of *Tales of Soldiers and Civilians* began appearing in the pages of Hearst's *Examiner* and other newspapers. Aside from the rhapsodic style of the passage quoted above, the paragraph is significant for its sense of poignant contrast between former beauty and present ugliness, its apostrophy to "Youth" as the time when life was "gracious and picturesque," and the nostalgic tone of regret that such moments can come no more.

Still more significant is the fact that there are several styles and "tones" in "What I Saw of Shiloh." The lyrical strain is restricted mainly to a kind of coda that follows the end of the battle descriptions. The essay opens on an entirely different note: "This is a simple story of a battle; such a tale as may be told by a soldier who is no writer to a reader who is no soldier." While Bierce does considerable straight reporting, the essay is no "simple story" and Bierce is very much the writer in striving for particular effects. For example, he tells us that "the flag flapped excitedly, shaking out its blazonry of stars and stripes with a sort of fierce delight"; or that a bugle call "goes to the heart as wine and stirs the blood like the kisses of a beautiful woman." At other times he is whimsical, ironic, or starkly matter of fact. The point is that Bierce seems unable to maintain any consistent point of view toward his experience. Near the middle of the essay he tells the reader that "in subordination to the design of this narrative" the "incidents related necessarily group themselves about my own personality as a center." [12] The problem, however, is that Bierce's own personality responds to what he is describing in several ways. Sometimes he appears to be outside the action entirely, viewing it panoramically, almost historically; at other times the style becomes impressionistic as Bierce strives for an effect of intense immediacy. The center is always shifting. Although the lyrical coda at the end tells us some important things about Bierce's attitudes, it fails to draw the essay together. In fact, as we shall see presently, it is rudely contradicted by certain passages in the essay itself.

In "On a Mountain," the opening essay of "Bits of Autobiography," Bierce tells of his early army days in West Virginia. It was apparently written much later than "What I Saw of Shiloh" for he is "looking back upon it through the haze of near half a century." The area was the Cheat Mountain country, but Bierce always referred to it as the "Delectable Mountains," "a veritable realm of enchantment." [13] What he responds to most is the natural beauty of the place—the fragrance of spruce and pine, the bracing mountain air, the unfamiliar hills and valleys:

How romantic it all was; the sunset valleys full of visible sleep; the glades suffused and interpenetrated with moonlight; the long valley of the Greenbrier stretching away to we knew not what silent cities; the river itself unseen under its "astral body" of mist! [14]

Because it is much shorter than the Shiloh essay, and written later, "On a Mountain" is a more successfully handled piece of writing. For one thing, its tone is usually under control. From the perspective of almost fifty years, Bierce describes with amused irony his days as a patriotic and naïve recruit, away from home for the first time and exhilarated by his new surroundings.

While there is nothing extraordinary about a man's softening and romanticizing some exciting period of his youth, Bierce's almost compulsive preoccupation with his army years suggests a mind unable to develop along with new experiences and changing circumstances. Bierce's famous misanthropy hints at a man profoundly dissatisfied not only with his era but with himself. It is for this reason that his return to the old battlefields is as meaningful as the disappearance that followed shortly after.[15] In a letter to an unnamed correspondent, Bierce wrote what is perhaps the most revealing statement of his attitude toward his service days:

I have told her of a certain "enchanted forest" hereabout to which I feel myself sometimes strongly drawn as a fitting place to lay down "my weary body and my head." . . .

The element of enchantment in that forest is supplied by my wandering and dreaming in it forty-one years ago when I was a-soldiering and there were new things under a new sun. It is miles away, but from a near-by summit I can overlook the entire region—ridge beyond ridge, parted by purple valleys full of sleep. . . . Can you guess my feelings when I view this Dream-land—my Realm of Adventure, inhabited by memories that beckon me from every valley? I shall go; I shall retrace my old routes and lines of march; stand in my old camps; inspect my battle-fields to see that all is right and undisturbed. I shall go to the Enchanted Forest.[16]

Although Bierce never ceased to view the war days through a romantic haze or to extol this period as the culmination of his life, he encountered other experiences in the "Enchanted Forest" of a far different nature, ones he was never able to reconcile himself to. These experiences he could treat in no other way than realistically and with a grim irony that suggests how deeply his sensibility was involved. In the final paragraph of "What I Saw of Shiloh" (quoted above), Bierce wonders why he could so vividly remember "all that was gracious and picturesque," whereas he could only "recall with difficulty the danger and death and horrors of the time." Such a statement is an interesting evasion. It is belied not only by the starkly graphic detail with which he describes death and its attendant horrors in "What I Saw of Shiloh," but by the concern with death and suffering that dominates his fiction. There is nothing facetious in his definition of "longevity" as an "uncommon extension of the fear of death," [17] nor was Bierce being merely witty when he wrote:

> "I think," says the philosopher divine,
> "Therefore I am." Sir, here's a surer sign:
> We know we live, for with our very breath
> We feel the fear, and imminence of death.[18]

In "What I Saw of Shiloh" Bierce recreates two separate encounters with death with a chilling authority that shows he remembered such things more readily than he admitted. In the first description Bierce has been inspecting the scene of a savage battle the day before:

> There were men enough; all dead, apparently, except one, who lay near where I had halted my platoon to await the slower movement of the line—a Federal sergeant, variously hurt, who had been a fine giant in his time. He lay face upward, taking in his breath in convulsive, rattling snorts, and blowing it out in sputters of froth which crawled creamily down his cheeks, piling itself alongside his neck and ears. A bullet had clipped a groove in his skull, above the temple; from this the brain protruded in bosses, dropping off in flakes and strings.[19]

At this point, instead of letting the description speak for itself, Bierce does something typical of his least successful writing: he tries to make an ironic joke of the matter, as if to reassure himself that he is under perfect control. Thus he observes: "I had not previously known one could get on, even in this unsatisfactory fashion, with so little brain."[20] The remark is both pointless and in bad taste, but the very fact Bierce felt impelled to make it is significant. What he apparently wanted to do was to convince the reader that such grisly sights did not affect *him:*

> One of my men, whom I knew for a womanish fellow, asked if he should put his bayonet through him. Inexpressibly shocked by the cold-blooded proposal, I told him I thought not; it was unusual, and too many were looking.[21]

But it is really the Federal sergeant and not the proposal of the "womanish" companion that has "inexpressibly shocked" Bierce.

The other encounter with death and horror is even more frightening. Having obtained permission to visit a small valley where the battle had been followed by a fierce forest fire, Bierce descended to where "death had put his sickle into this thicket and fire had gleaned the field." [22] There he found the bodies of the wounded who had been burned to death.

Their clothing was half burnt away—their hair and beard entirely; the rain had come too late to save their nails. Some were swollen to double girth; others shriveled to manikins. According to degree of exposure, their faces were bloated and black or yellow and shrunken. The contraction of muscles which had given them claws for hands had cursed each countenance with a hideous grin.[23]

The precise detail implies how deeply such an encounter had etched itself on Bierce's memory, and that he had likely spent considerable time studying these postures of agony. The experience meant more to him than is suggested by his concluding remark: "Faugh! I cannot catalogue the charms of these gallant gentlemen who had got what they enlisted for." [24]

Sometimes Bierce juxtaposes two antithetical responses and attitudes, as if he wished to achieve the maximum contrast. For example, in "On a Mountain," the paragraph describing the "sunset valleys full of sleep," the "romantic" "Greenbrier stretching away to we knew not what silent cities," is followed by this experience:

As we trudged on we passed something—some things—

lying by the wayside. During another wait we examined them, curiously lifting the blankets from their yellow-clay faces. How repulsive they looked with their blood-smears, their blank, staring eyes, their teeth uncovered by contraction of the lips! The frost had begun already to whiten their deranged clothing. We were as patriotic as ever, but we did not wish to be that way.[25]

It is worth noting that here, unlike the passage about the Federal sergeant, Bierce makes no attempt to dramatize himself as the hardened veteran, nor does he give us the nervously facetious remark. His subdued understatement captures perfectly the impact of death's face upon a group of raw recruits. But Bierce cannot seem to leave the dead alone, and spoils his effect in the very next paragraph. Passing the same corpses the next day, "feeble from fatigue and savage from defeat," Bierce notices "that these bodies had altered their position": "They appeared also to have thrown off some of their clothing, which lay near by, in disorder. Their expression, too, had an added blankness—they had no faces." Later he discovers the cause: "a herd of galloping swine" which some indignant soldiers are firing at. "They had eaten our fallen, but—touching magnanimity!—we did not eat theirs." Bierce then concludes "On a Mountain" on a note of sophomoric gaiety: "The shooting of several kinds was very good in the Cheat Mountain country, even in 1861." [26]

In the war stories death is described with the same starkly precise detail, the same sense of awful finality, that we find in Bierce's essays on his experiences as a soldier. The principal difference in presentation, however, is that in the stories, Bierce spares us the disruptive flippancy, the grim little joke designed to assure us of his own detachment. Whereas in the essays "events necessarily group themselves about [his] own personality as a center," in the stories Bierce maintains an objective point of view. Like Poe, whose aesthetic principles he follows, Bierce believed in the impersonality of the artist, and what one writer has said of Poe can be applied to Bierce as well:

Poe . . . perceived the essential impersonality of the real artist; and knew that the function of creative fiction is merely to express and interpret events and sensations as they are, regardless of how they tend or what they prove —good or evil, attractive or repulsive, stimulating or depressing, with the author always acting as a vivid and detached chronicler rather than as a teacher, sympathizer, or vender of opinion.[27]

Death comes in many forms in the war tales. Sometimes it is as swift and mysterious as the bullet Private Grayrock fired in the dark forest, killing his beloved brother; sometimes it is as peaceful as the general's quiet exit in "Parker Adderson, Philosopher." In "George Thurston," the protagonist dies "an ignoble death": "Thurston's body lay on its back. One leg, bent beneath, was broken above the knee and the bone driven into the earth. The abdomen had burst; the bowels protruded. The neck was broken." To Captain Graffenreid, under fire for the first time and forced to take cover behind a corpse, the face of death "looked yellow already, and was repulsive," and "nothing suggested the glory of a soldier's death nor mitigated the loathsomeness of the incident." It is the violence of Graffenreid's encounter with death—its sudden, senseless reality—that jars him out of all his comfortable illusions about life and about himself and leads to his suicide. This is why the horrors Bierce describes in the war stories are seldom merely gratuitous; they are the inevitable corollaries of his vision. To Bierce, existence was an essentially destructive, rather than creative, process, not only because it led to the meaninglessness of death, but also because experience taught the futility of all human hopes and ideals. Once such illusions have been systematically exposed, what remains is the paralyzing horror at the heart of things—the terrible emptiness of life itself. It is this fundamental conception that governs the action and imagery of Bierce's parable, "Chickamauga"; what the child is left with at the end can only be defined in naturalistic terms:

> There, conspicuous in the light of the conflagration, lay the dead body of a woman—the white face turned upward, the hands thrown out and clutched full of grass, the clothing deranged, the long dark hair in tangles and full of clotted blood. The greater part of the forehead was torn away, and from the jagged hole the brain protruded, overflowing the temple, a frothy mass of gray, crowned with clusters of crimson bubbles—the work of a shell.

The war stories are oppressively nihilistic because Bierce postulates a world in which empirical reality is always demolishing the products of the creative imagination. Idealistic assumptions about life are continually being undermined by the destructive nature of experience, until the only assumption worth holding, according to Bierce, is that "nothing matters." Whether this process takes place gradually, as it apparently did in Bierce's own life, or with dramatic suddenness, as in the stories, the result is the same: a wreck of shattered dreams about personal happiness and achievement, about ideal values and virtues, about the rich possibilities of life itself. Does Parker Adderson imagine his readings in the stoic philosophers have made him impervious to the fear of death? Send him out to be executed tonight instead of in the morning as he expects, and watch his reaction. Does Jerome Searing assume that his bravery and professional competence are equal to any demands? Let a shell demolish his hiding place and show him the trap of his human limitations. Does the deaf-mute in "Chickamauga" view life as an endless game of easy conquest? Have him gaze upon the body of his mother so that the "little world" of his childish imagination is turned around and the "points of the compass" "reversed." In essence, this is the focal point of Bierce's well-known bitterness: a stultifying awareness of the promise of life betrayed by its actual conditions.

Because Bierce concentrates his effects on the "moment of truth," the sinister event that kills the spirit if not the body, the promise of life is seldom developed with any dramatic intensity. In "One Officer, One Man," for example, Graffenreid's erroneous beliefs about himself and the possibilities of heroic achievement are described in a few brief paragraphs; the main part of the story is concerned with the psychological pressures that drive him to suicide. Jerome Searing's interior life in "One of the Missing" consists of a series of deteriorating responses to his dilemma; we simply infer an original faith in his own self-sufficiency. In "Chickamauga," however, Bierce uses a somewhat different technique. The actions and scenes of the story are described both objectively and as they are viewed through the child's myopic vision. The result is a grotesque incongruity between the actual circumstances and the way matters appear to the child. Only at the final moment are perception and judgment correctly aligned. But the more usual procedure with Bierce is to "assume" without demonstration that the protagonist, invariably young and untried, has assumptions about life that ignore its painful realities.

It is for this reason that Bierce's curiously ambivalent attitude toward his own war experience is significant. Although, as we have seen, he describes his encounters with death and horror as unsparingly as he does in the stories, such matters appear in the war essays almost incidentally. They are disturbing interludes in what Bierce seems to have regarded as a period of high adventure. Often he reacts to war's humorous side, or to the natural beauty of his surroundings; he always writes with a keen sense of living fully and intensely. We seldom catch any hint of the despairing fatalism of the war tales, their pervasive feeling of life's emptiness. In fact, the strongest impression these essays make is of an almost irrepressible euphoria, a glowing self-confidence. This is why Bierce writes so nostalgically at the end of "What I Saw of Shiloh"; he is overcome by the contrast between the "magic spell" of "those days of youth" and the "harsher features of this later world," the "ugliness of the longer and tamer life." After describing the romantic memories that pass before his vision, Bierce shifts to the ominous present:

Here in the night stretches a wide and blasted field studded with half-extinct fires burning redly with I know not what presage of evil. Again I shudder as I note its desolation and its awful silence. Where was it? To what monstrous inharmony of death was it the visible prelude?

It is by no means clear what Bierce is driving at here. What is clear, however, is that something went fatally wrong with his own youthful expectations, something that turned *his* world around and reversed the points of the compass.

The sometimes overwrought lyricism of the war essays reflects Bierce's attempt to recapture that moment in his youth when his enthusiasm and idealistic expectations were at their highest. It is not the war itself Bierce is romanticizing, but what he takes to be his poignant separation from that "Golden Age" when "there were new things under a new sun." Since he regards the present time as without hope or meaning, and thus the true human condition, the past is characteristically described as a cherished dream-state, to be evoked periodically by simple memory or, more significantly, by revisiting old battlefields. When he is most rhapsodic, it is because he is thinking of the past as "the Future of yesterday"; [28] that is, he is most aware of it as the period before his own frustration and disillusionment. The fluctuations of tone and style in these essays mirror his wavering attitude. As a man with a strong romantic impulse, he wanted to indulge in daydreams of youthful adventure and promise, but at the same time he knew they were as empty as the present actuality he was trying to turn away from.

Although all of Bierce's war stories play variations

on a single theme, some reveal more clearly than others Bierce's defeated idealism. One such story is "The Mocking-bird," which has already been discussed in connection with the theme of an inscrutably destructive universe. In its actions and images "The Mocking-bird" can also be regarded as a parable of Bierce's lost illusions. Whether the entire story is an unconscious symbolic representation is hard to say. There is some evidence, however, that it is, and that several of Bierce's most deeply felt attitudes are embedded in the matrix of the story. Like the song of the mockingbird itself, the story has a tantalizing ambiguity about it that suggests something more than a variation on the trite theme of divided kinsmen.

The action of "The Mocking-bird" takes place on a deceptively "pleasant Sunday afternoon in the early autumn of 1861" when "the war was young." William Grayrock, whose character "was a singularly felicitous compound of boldness and sensibility, courage and conscience," is lost in thought in "a forest's heart." The previous night, Grayrock was literally lost while on picket duty. "In the gloom of the wood the darkness was deep," and when he found himself completely disoriented, "Grayrock was profoundly disquieted." Firing at the "indistinct outlines of a human figure," Grayrock stampedes the other green recruits into a mad dash back to camp. Only because he does not know which way to go, Grayrock stands his ground and is subsequently praised for his "bravery." Grayrock's "sensibility" makes him want to find the man he is sure he killed since he feels guilty about receiving unmerited commendation. Telling the sentinel "that he had lost something," he returns on Sunday to the scene of his strange experience the night before. But Grayrock can find nothing, and seating himself at the base of a large pine tree, he "indulged his disappointment."

So far the story has no clearly defined symbolic contour, although there is something that suggests Bierce's own problems in Grayrock's compulsive return to the scene of a baffling experience, as well as in the motif of disorientation. It is when Grayrock falls asleep ("and sleeping he dreamed") that "The Mocking-bird" begins to assume some richer overtones. Perhaps the most striking feature of Grayrock's dream in the forest is the close similarity between its images and those Bierce used at the conclusion of "What I Saw of Shiloh" and in his letter explaining why he must go back to the "enchanted forest" of his youth. Like Bierce, Grayrock dreams of a former period of rich promise, when he and his twin brother John stood gazing at "the Realm of Conjecture" and "caught glimpses of the Enchanted Land." It was a happy time when there were "new things under a new sun," and the song of their pet mockingbird "seemed . . . the spirit of the scene, the meaning and interpretation to sense of the mysteries of life and love." What Bierce apparently meant by the phrase "to sense" is that those "golden days" were a time when life was experienced sensuously rather than rationally or intellectually. The bird only *seemed* to define an age of joy and promise. Later, when William wakes from his dream and sees a real mockingbird, he cries when it pours "from its joyous breast so inexhaustible floods of song as but one of all God's creatures can utter in His praise." But the bird is deceptive—a mockingbird in earnest as it turns out —and the undeceived narrator remarks of its singing: "There was little in that—it was only to open the bill and breathe." The song, however, has overwhelmed Grayrock and "for the moment he was, indeed, a child, in spirit and in memory . . . ." His emotions and his imagination have tricked him into an unjustified assumption of the bird's significance, just as its song in his childhood had seemed to tell of joy and the "mysteries of life and love." "With an effort of will he pulled himself together, . . . and audibly damning himself for an idiot strode on."

Grayrock's dream—the fact that this happy time was only a dream is perhaps the main point—is dominated by the mockingbird's "musical benediction." "But there came a time when the days of the dream grew dark," the home was "broken up," and the brothers, identical twins, were separated. William, "the dreamer," went to live in the "Realm of Conjecture" and John, who had inherited the mockingbird, went "into the Enchanted Land." When Grayrock wakes, the sun is ominously "low and red in the west" and casts a "wall of shadow" across "the golden haze to eastward." The shadow that falls across "the golden haze" is, of course, William's horrifying discovery that he had killed his brother the night before, the "image of himself" that he stumbles on in the "heart of the little thicket." "Flushed with sunset's crimson glory," the mockingbird "glided silently away through the solemn spaces of the wood."

It is possible that Bierce intended "The Mockingbird" to be nothing more than a strange tale of the irony of fate or circumstance. If so, the fantastic coincidence that causes William Grayrock to shoot his twin brother in the dark and then take his own life is neither convincing nor original. But the fatal encounter of the twins has a subtler kind of symbolic logic which appears to originate in Bierce's sense of his own lost youth and defeated ideals. For example, the overall pattern of the story is one of contrast between a destructive reality in the present time and a former period of youthful hope and joy defined in the richly suggestive language of a dream. This pattern we have previously encountered in Bierce's war essays and letters when he went "wandering and dreaming" in his own "enchanted forest," and "there were new things under a new sun." It was his "Dream-land," his "Realm of Adventure" and, like Grayrock's forest, "inhabited by memories."

Even more revealing is the contrast between the "Realm of Conjecture," where William went to live, and the "Enchanted Land," where John made his home. William's home suggests both the actual world of the immediate present and William's tendency to theorize about life, to draw conclusions from its uncertain premises. John's mysterious "Enchanted Land" is a nonexistent dream-state, a "distant region," to which William returns momentarily when he becomes a child "in spirit and in memory." Its deceptive reality is "to sense" only, just as the mockingbird is a false prophet of joyous promise. Significantly, it is immediately *after* William pulls himself together "with an effort of the will"—that is, returns to the world of actuality and the exercise of his rational faculties—that he finds the dead "image of himself." The inevitable has happened; the childish dream of life's joy and fullness, a product of the creative imagination, has been demolished by an empirical knowledge of the real world and its ways. It is not John who has been killed, but William's longing to believe in an enchanted land of bright promise and benevolent purpose. If the story expresses Bierce's impulse to recapture some lost period when life seemed purposeful and lovely, then the brothers are actually two aspects of Bierce himself which became "separated" during the war. Furthermore, the analytical, conjectural Bierce, who tried to see life realistically, unintentionally "killed" Bierce the romantic idealist, who tried once to believe that life was exciting and good. Like all of Bierce's war stories, "The Mocking-bird" is concerned with the emptiness of dreams.

Bierce, always an admirer of Poe, may have gotten a clue for his use of identical twins from Poe's story of divided personality, "William Wilson." [29] The motif of coming upon one's own dead body has various sources and analogues, most notably a recurrent dream Bierce had as a young man and which he describes in an essay called "Visions of the Night." [30] In this dream Bierce is struggling over a landscape that suggests the setting of "Childe Roland." He reaches a gigantic building with countless doors and passageways through which he wanders aimlessly, coming finally to a tiny room at the end of a long corridor. There, on a slab, lies a sheeted corpse; when Bierce raises the sheet he is horrified to find himself staring down at his own body. The corpse is shriveled, but the blue eyes are wide open and regard the visitor tranquilly. Perhaps the real meaning of "The Mocking-bird" is implied in a remark Bierce once made to his friend Walter Neale. Bierce had been discussing his belief that each individual was not one personality, but a combination of multiple personalities, each representing different stages of emotional or intellectual development. What he was trying to prove was the unlikelihood of human immortality, since it was inconceivable that these multiple identities, acquired at various times, could all survive. Of his own case he observed: "When I ask myself what has become of Ambrose Bierce the youth, who fought at Chickamauga, I am bound to answer that he is dead." [31] And so he was. There in the enchanted forest he "lost something" that he never recovered, although he went back over the same ground many times to find it.

The gulf separating appearance from reality, past from present, the dreams of life from its actual conditions, is a measure of Bierce's thwarted idealism and romantic undercurrents. Caught between an impulse to idealize and romanticize experience and an equally strong impulse to see things exactly as they are, Bierce often wrote in the aggrieved manner of a man who had been betrayed. In the *Examiner* (May 9, 1897), Bierce comments bitterly on the collapse of his faith in moral principle:

Time was, in that far fair world of youth where I went a-soldiering for Freedom, when the moral character of every thought and word and deed was determined by reference to a set of infinitely precious "principles"—infallible criteria—moral solvents, mordant to all base metals, and warranted by the manufacturers and vendors to disclose the gold in every proposition submitted to its tenets. I have no longer the advantage of their service, but must judge everything on its own merits—each case as it comes up.[32]

As the language suggests, Bierce writes as if he had been gypped at some traveling medicine show and was determined it would never happen again.

He was always feeling that he had been let down—by his friends, his publishers, his own expectations, and life itself. "I'm beginning to cherish an impertinent curiosity to know what Heaven means to do to me next," he once wrote in reference to the failure of his New York publishers.[33] Always on the lookout for some new disappointment, he seemed to develop a talent for finding it. Like many sensitives, Bierce constructed elaborate defenses against the assaults of his own emotions. He was brusque and aloof, and often irritatingly dogmatic and pontifical in expressing his opinions. As a further defense, he elaborated a theory that emotion was injurious to the writer and that the intellect should always act as stern censor of the feelings. He belittled religion because it was "a matter, not of reason, but of feeling—not of the head, but of the heart," and preferred to think that his was a "mind congenitally gifted with the power of logic and accessible to its light and leading." In his essay "To Train a Writer," Bierce outlines a rigorous five-year course; during the first two years, the neophyte would never put pen to paper. Bierce would have this time devoted to "teaching him how to think and giving him something to think about—to sharpening his faculties of observation, *dispelling his illusions and destroying his ideals*" (italics added). The apprentice would be taught that "in the virtues, so-called, he should discern only the rough notes of a general expediency." [34] In short, Bierce would make him what he thought himself to be: "rational," "devoid of all delusions save those of observation, experience and reflection." [35]

Bierce seems to have been bent on convincing himself that ideals had no real meaning, that there were no principles except those of expediency and, therefore, that they had no power to hurt or disappoint.[36] They were the products of an idle fancy and emotional wishful thinking. As his writing clearly shows, he came to feel that all painful emotions could be laughed and mocked out of existence. That such a strategy convinced some people is shown by the frequent charge of "inhumanity" leveled at Bierce's work. But Bierce was hardly inhuman, and his intellect never subverted his heart, although he prided himself on some sort of Olympian tragic vision, of looking down from "the dominating peaks austere and desolate" and "holding a prophecy of doom." [37] In fact, in a letter of rebuke to some friend who had apparently not lived up to Bierce's expectations, he warned:

> And let me tell you that if you are going through life as a mere thinking machine, ignoring the generous promptings of the heart, sacrificing it to the brain, you will have a hard row to hoe, and the outcome, when you survey it from the vantage ground of age, will not please you.[38]

No one knew better than Bierce the price one had to pay to rationalize one's disappointments.

Because he could never resolve the conflicting impulses within himself, Bierce went through life with a severe case of *Weltschmerz.* One suspects that he may have consciously cultivated it, but despite a tendency toward self-dramatization, there is no doubt that Bierce felt things deeply, most of all his own frustrations. His friend and protégé, Herman Scheffauer, has said of him:

> He was saved from the sterility and the superficiality of the true cynic by the tragic undercurrents of his nature. . . . He was still able to grieve with sorrow, and to sympathize with suffering, though ever on his guard against encroachments of his heart upon his head.[39]

And in a similar vein, another friend observed: "in spite of that cold aloofness which he contended to be the true attitude of the artist, occasionally he would give a glimpse of the compassion he really felt for war's victims." [40] Bierce doubtlessly sympathized with "war's victims," but more important, he saw himself as one of war's most poignant casualties, and his best tales are those in which his own dilemmas are most completely involved.

One of Bierce's most popular war stories, frequently anthologized, is "A Son of the Gods." [41] Subtitled "A Study in the Present Tense," it differs in several important respects from the rest of Bierce's fiction. It is written in an emotionally heightened style quite unlike the detached and austere manner typical of his fiction as a whole. In fact, McWilliams finds "A Son of the Gods" "romanticized to an unbelievable degree," [42] and seems to dismiss the story as a piece of rhetorical theatrics. But the fact that the story is highly mannered is itself a clue to its meaning, for it is as much the quality of the narrator's response to events as the events themselves that Bierce is concerned with. Unnamed, like all the characters, the narrator exists to articulate the emotional reactions of a group of passive spectators referred to usually as "we." In particular, he is the spokesman for a point of view that is bitterly mocked at the end of the story. By using the present tense throughout, Bierce creates a feeling of intense immediacy and empathic absorption which gives the story a curiously static, tableau-like effect. It is not a narrative in time that is aimed at, but a state of mind. Moreover, the subtitle, "A Study in the Present Tense," is pointedly ironic. As a projection of Bierce's original belief in life's heroic possibilities, "A Son of the Gods" goes back in time to recreate both the moment of belief and the conditions that made belief impossible. Bierce implies that the romantic style of the story as a whole, as well as the emotional fervor of the narrator, can only be justified by turning the past into the present.

According to evidence in one of Bierce's newspaper columns, the main plot situation in "A Son of the Gods" derives from an experience in which Bierce himself was the principal figure. He tells of the time he was sent with some reserve troops to help a brigade whose flank had become dangerously exposed. Without orders, he decided to find out how the enemy was deployed.

> I never felt so brave in all my life. I rode a hundred yards in advance, prepared to expostulate single handed with the victorious enemy at whatever point I might encounter him. I dashed forward through every open space into every suspicious looking wood and spurred to the crest of every hill, exposing myself recklessly to draw the

Confederate fire and disclose their position. I told the commander of the relief column that he need not throw out any advance guard as a precaution against the ambuscade—I would myself act in that perilous capacity. . . .[43]

Although Bierce was cited later for bravery, his act turned out to be without value, since the danger had passed and the reserves had been recalled.

In "A Son of the Gods," Bierce's reckless courage becomes the property of a dashing young officer "on a snow-white horse," and Bierce becomes the narrator, an enthralled spectator of selfless heroism who identifies himself only as a "staff officer." He is part of a large force of Federal troops, poised at the edge of a wood while studying the crest of a hill a mile ahead across dangerously open country. Along the ridge of the hill runs a stone wall backed by a heavy growth of hedge and trees. "Among the trees—what? It is necessary to know." Tracks across the open fields show that the enemy has passed recently in the direction of the ominous hill; the vital question is whether they have moved on or lie in wait to cut down the hesitating army. Ordinarily, a skirmish line would be sent ahead to test the enemy's strength, but just as the commander gives such an order, the young officer gallops up. He appears to be making some kind of request: "Let us ride a little nearer. Ah! too late—it is ended." The officer then "wheels his horse, and rides straight toward the crest of the hill!"

Since the story's meaning is found in the narrator's responses to the officer's spectacular deed, it is important to note them carefully. Paradoxically, Bierce's uncertainty of response, which we noted in the war essays and which becomes a major symptom of his problem as a writer, has a functional value in "A Son of the Gods." For example, at first he and the others regard the officer as either stupid or impossibly vain. "What a fool!" says the narrator of the hero's conspicuous white horse and scarlet blanket, and as the officer rides up to the corps commander "a wave of derisive laughter runs abreast of him all along the line." At the same time, the narrator is strongly stirred by his gallant bearing:

> This young officer is in full uniform, as if on parade. He is all agleam with bullion—a blue-and-gold edition of the Poetry of War. . . . But how handsome he is!—with what careless grace he sits his horse!

As the officer rides "at a walk, straight up the long slope," "ten thousand pairs of eyes" watch fascinated, and the derisive laughter gives way to unstinting admiration. "How glorious! Gods! What would we not give to be in his place—with his soul!" The observers are "hardened and impenitent man-killers" who see death's face daily, but now they are caught up, "with suspended breath and beating hearts," in one man's act. "Such is the magnetism of courage and devotion." Time and movement appear to cease in the intensity of the moment: "Not a word is spoken," the corps commander turns into "an equestrian statue of himself," the other officers, "their field-glasses up, are motionless all."

To the narrator, the officer appears mysteriously symbolic, bent on making a sacrificial offering of himself to save the skirmish line. He notes the sunshine that glints upon his shoulder straps "lovingly, like a visible benediction" and wishes he would look back at his comrades to "see the love, the adoration, the atonement!" He is "this gallant man—this military Christ!" As the narrator watches through field glasses he begins to realize that the officer is doomed unless the hedgerow proves deserted. If the enemy is entrenched, and is seen, then some sniper will bring him down long before he can return with the news. He could allow himself to be captured, but "this would defeat his object . . . it is necessary either that he return unharmed or be shot to death before our eyes. Only so shall we know how to act." Suddenly the solitary horseman turns and gallops parallel to the wall: "He has caught sight of his antagonist; he knows all." But the enemy shrewdly holds its fire while the officer gallops up and down the line trying to make them shoot and thus disclose their size and deployment to his comrades. Only by a series of charges directly at the wall does he manage to start an infectious firing. He miraculously survives the first volley and when the smoke clears, "the enchanted horse and rider" are seen charging another segment of the hill "to unveil another conspiracy of silence, to thwart the will of another armed host."

To enhance a feeling of intense immediacy—of presence—Bierce has his narrator address the reader as if he, too, were there and the aesthetic distance did not exist: "but take this field-glass and you will observe that he is riding toward a break in the wall and hedge." The "we" expands to include all those who respond to "the magnetism of courage and devotion" and believe in a world where heroism is both possible and meaningful. And so, when the officer, mortally wounded, his horse shot from under him, makes his last noble gesture, it takes on the character of a mystical communion between him and "ten thousand hearts":

He stands erect, motionless, holding his sabre in his right hand straight above his head. His face is turned toward us. Now he lowers his hand to a level with his face and moves it outward, the blade of the sabre describing a downward curve. It is a sign to us, to the world, to posterity. It is a hero's salute to death and history.

At this moment "the spell is broken"; the men "choking with emotion," begin "to press tumultuously forward into the open." Somehow, the officer's "salute to death and history" has so miraculously inspired the soldiers that "without orders, against orders," they launch an attack upon the hill. As "line after line sweeps forth, catching the sunlight on its burnished arms," the army appears to partake of the officer's own nobility. They are "like hounds unleashed"; the simile enforces the completely irrational, instinctive nature of their behavior. Like so many of Bierce's protagonists—and the ten thousand soldiers behave with a single consciousness—the soldiers do not so much act as react, in this case to a series of emotionally explosive stimuli. By the same token, the narrator's rhapsodic tone defines both his own commitment and that of the others to the heroic ideal of their "military Christ."

When the officer begins his series of spectacular charges against the enemy wall, the narrator addresses the reader with a warning: "You are not to forget the nature of this man's act; it is not permitted to you to think of it as an instance of bravado, nor, on the other hand, a needless sacrifice of self." The remark is ambiguously ironic. In the first place, it is belied by the action itself, for once the inspired army moves from the forest into the open fields, it is met by a murderous fire from the crest of the hill, and many are killed. The selfless act of the young officer, intended to sacrifice one life to save many, produces quite the opposite effect. On the other hand, it is clear where the narrator's sympathies lie, so that his remark, quoted above, is not mere cynicism. Presumably the narrator, as a staff officer, is caught in the middle, so to speak; he is inspired by what he sees, but significantly, he refers to the soldiers as "they" instead of "we" when they launch their attack. He has somehow detached himself and now stands apart from the suicidal rush at the hill.

It is not suggested that the narrator's problem of finding the "correct" point of view is a part of the story's design. The narrator serves only to reflect a kind of response to the hero's deed. He is not an independently significant character in his own right; that is, we do not care about what he *does*, only what he *feels*. If the narrator has a problem of ambivalent attitudes, Bierce keeps it carefully in the background and makes it clear that the narrator is profoundly moved by all that takes place. The "problem" is really tangential to the story proper, since it consists of Bierce's own civil war between his head and his heart, his rational faculties and his yearning for rich imaginative and emotional experience. As the real-life source for the story's hero, Bierce was emotionally involved in his frustrated sacrifice, but at the same time concerned with giving his experience a larger significance. Thus the narrator embodies Bierce's attempt to identify himself with the idealistic Bierce who "died" at Chickamauga and also to see the matter with a certain detachment. Using the present tense recaptures a former point of view with all its emotional reverberations; the numerous references to looking through field glasses suggest Bierce's desire to find the proper "focus," the right combination of nearness to, and distance from, the experience he describes.

Although the narrator does not appear to move with the inspired soldiers, this is not something called to our attention. Bierce's own tendency to view life realistically, to regard "principles" as a matter of expediency and ideals and emotions with distrust, is objectified in the commander of the "insurgent" troops. He is the figure who ordered the skirmish line brought up at the beginning of the story, but he does not reappear until the next to last paragraph. While the soldiers press forward he "has not moved"; he coolly observes "the human current flowing on either side of him . . . like tide waves parted by a rock." Since our own responses as readers are necessarily keyed to that of the narrator, a would-be believer in the heroic ideal, there is something irritating—almost sinister—in the commander's complete detachment. In fact, the most remarkable thing about him is that there is "not a sign of feeling in his face; he is thinking." He is as deliberate and reflective in his actions as the troops are emotional and irrational in theirs and, not moving, he is unmoved as well. Significantly, he puts away his field glasses so that he can get a more comprehensive view of things, a view that results in his order to sound retreat. The army which moments before swept forth "catching the sunlight on its burnished arms" now returns to the wood "slowly," "sullenly," "bearing their wounded," gathering their dead. The dream of glory and noble achievement has once more given way to a painful and frustrating reality.

The commander, however, is not the villain of the piece. He seems sinister because he displays no emotion whatsoever, like the "thinking machine" Bierce warned a friend he might become if he ignored the "generous promptings of the heart." As a highly fluid symbol, the commander gathers up and concentrates several of Bierce's most important ideas and attitudes. For example, he is reason itself, destroyer of beautiful illusions, and at the same time the harsh reality of the human condition in which expediency replaces principle, and men live not nobly, but "sullenly." He has the shock value of a bad-tasting medicine—bitterly unpleasant but therapeutic. Viewed in this way, the commander symbolizes the rational faculties which must purge excessive emotion. As a military leader, he is the embodiment of order, sanity, and discipline, threatened for a time by the insubordination of his troops, but able to reassert his proper authority. Since his order to withdraw saves his men from further needless slaughter, from that "malign and awful hill," he suggests Bierce's capitulation to things as they are. On the other hand, Bierce found it extremely hard to accept the defeat of his dream. As the narrator observes ruefully:

> Ah, those many, many needless dead! That great soul whose beautiful body is lying over yonder, so conspicuous

against the sere hillside—could it not have been spared the bitter consciousness of a vain devotion? Would one exception have marred too much the pitiless perfection of the divine, eternal plan?

Perhaps Bierce thought of the figure on the hillside, like the body of John Grayrock in "The Mockingbird," as another "image of himself" that had died in the war; the man who lived on wrote "A Son of the Gods" with "the bitter consciousness of a vain devotion."

"A Son of the Gods" is both a successful story and an important one for understanding the romantic and idealistic strains in Bierce. Artistically, the story brings his own conflicting impulses under control by objectifying them in the antithetical figures of the narrator and the commander and in the ambiguously ironic young officer. If, as McWilliams says, the incidents are "romanticized to an unbelievable degree," Bierce clearly intended them to be, for his narrator had high expectations and was bitterly disillusioned. In the final paragraph, Bierce makes it plain that no one was really to blame: not the young officer, nor the watching soldiers he so mystically inspired, not even the commander who was as powerless as any. The cause lay somewhere in the incomprehensible constitution of things, as it invariably does in the war tales, for Bierce was always seeking to raise his idiosyncratic dilemmas and frustrations into a doctrine of fatalism and universal pessimism. War was the most compelling action to symbolize his beliefs since it placed the individual at the mercy of forces he could not control or understand. The principal symbolic action of "A Son of the

Gods," for example, is Bierce's archetypal movement from advance and expectation to disillusionment and retreat. No one can follow the mystical hero; reason shows this to be impossible. As in several of Bierce's stories, the forest to which the soldiers are forced to withdraw "sullenly" is the scene of their depressing understanding that if man is "a son of the gods," he is only a "humble, unheroic Prometheus," capable only of suffering and defeat, never of glory.

In going back to war's actions and images for the best fiction he ever wrote, Bierce was not simply drawing upon his own experiences. By the time Bierce began writing his tales, the war itself had crystallized into a symbol combining his youthful expectations of life and his postwar disillusionment. His perspective was one conscious of the distance between what once had *seemed* and what now *was*, between a sensuous involvement in experience and a detached contemplation of its limiting conditions. It is this perspective, in turn, which determines the symbolic action of Bierce's plots. The inward sense of impoverishment and frustration is externalized as some form of death or defeat which comes upon the protagonist through no fault of his own. He is carried along relentlessly by a whimsical destiny which propels him from illusions and false assumptions about life to a situation that points up the disparity between the knowledge and the dream. The success of the war tales generally lies in Bierce's ability to get outside himself sufficiently to objectify his own dilemma while at the same time his characters and their destructive experiences are close enough to be taken seriously and regarded with a measure of compassion.

Chapter III

A DIVIDED SENSIBILITY: POLARITIES OF RESPONSE TO ART AND LIFE

THE STRONG UNDERCURRENTS of a frustrated romantic idealism that run through all of Bierce's war stories become still more apparent when viewed in the light of his attitude toward art and literature in general. While his opinions on such matters are neither original nor profound, they are relevant to any consideration of Bierce's achievement as a short story writer. For one thing, they go a long way toward explaining why his career in fiction was so short-lived, despite his undeniable talents. Furthermore, they show how irrevocably Bierce's sensibilities were divided between a dogged faith in the primacy of the creative imagination and an equally determined effort to approach life "devoid of all delusions save those of observation, experience and reflection." It was Bierce the realist, writer of cynical skeptical journalism, who finally subverted Bierce the romantic dreamer of the "enchanted forest" and virtually ended his career in fiction. His war stories, recurrent dramas of his own divided allegiance, portray the split through their symbolic images and actions which define the distance between romantic dreams about life and its harshly reductive realities of death, defeat, or paralyzing frustration. But this same pattern also manifests itself in Bierce's use, in the tales, of two aesthetic techniques: one grimly naturalistic and matter-of-fact, the other emotionally heightened and highly imaginative. The combination of uncompromising realism and romantic extravagance, which has led more than one critic to despair of ever classifying Bierce's stories, makes more sense when seen in terms of his beliefs about art itself.

In a world where Bierce found little besides mediocrity and bad taste, cloying sentiment and the vulgar display of wealth and raw power, literature was the one value to which he could give his wholehearted support. In fact, reading through his scattered literary criticism, one gets the distinct impression that the romantic strain in Bierce, blocked in his fiction by his own disenchantment and denied any outlet in a stultifying age of crass materialism, released itself in his glorification of art. Nothing is so apparent in his criticism as his tendency to idealize art and literature and to idolize those who produced them. As he wrote in an essay called "Who Are Great?":

> Literature and art are about all that the world really cares for in the end; those who make them are not without justification in regarding themselves as masters in the House of Life and all others as their servitors.[1]

Bierce regarded art and literature as "the only things of permanent interest in this world,"[2] based upon principles "which are themselves eternal."[3] The emphasis upon art's permanence is significant, for it suggests Bierce's yearning for some kind of value or ideal that was impervious to change and time, safe from the deadening effect of prosaic reality. In fact, Bierce repeatedly stressed his belief that time was the only valid test of literary greatness, since posterity was free from any concern with the author's life or circumstances and judged works solely on their intrinsic merits.[4] Finding no significance or purpose in his existence, Bierce came to look upon art as "a clean, well-lighted place" where beauty, order, and meaning did exist.

Bierce's aesthetic beliefs, drawn largely from Poe, ultimately from Coleridge and romantic criticism in general, emphasize the supremacy of imagination. It was this faculty which made the true artist a king among men, for the writer "to whom life is not picturesque, enchanting, astonishing, terrible, is denied the gift and faculty divine, and being no poet can write no prose." [5] With the inward eye of imagination, however, the writer can paint the light that never was on sea or land:

> It is to him of widest knowledge, of deepest feeling, of sharpest observation and insight, that life is most crowded with figures of heroic stature, with spirits of dream, with demons of the pit, with graves that yawn in pathways leading to the light, with existences not of earth, both malign and benign—ministers of grace and ministers of doom. The truest eye is that which discerns the shadow and the portent, the dead hands reaching, the light that is the heart of the darkness, the sky "with dreadful faces thronged with fiery arms." [6]

Despite the somewhat blurry prose, the implications of the passage above are clear. The most significant point Bierce makes is that the great writer works with materials that have no tangible or finite existence, with nothing but the products of his own creative imagination. They are mysteriously insubstantial, "spirits of dream," "existences not of earth," "the shadow and the portent." What Bierce is most conscious of is the imagination's independence of everyday reality, its ability to carry the mind out of the actual conditions of human limitation. This idea is hardly new; its real importance lies in the appeal it held for Bierce. The language Bierce uses to describe the imagination's liberating power is very close to the language we find at the end of "What I Saw of Shiloh," in which a series of ghostly marvelous images pass before his vision. Although the war essays deal extensively with factual aspects of the war, especially when Bierce is describing death, the war experience as a whole is viewed through the same kind of romantic halo implied in the phrase, "the light that is the heart of the darkness." Such a light is the light of dreams, and everything that appealed most to Bierce about this period of his life is always described in terms of sleep and dreams. He went "dreaming" in the "enchanted forest," or its images "haunt" him, or it is his "Dream-land" "inhabited by memories." What all this suggests is that Bierce's own imagination, most operative in the war tales, was not so much creative in the fullest artistic sense as nostalgic, and depended heavily on a store of romantic memories about a particular experience. But the kind of dreams Bierce drew upon had long since proved deceptive when he began writing short stories, so that the stories themselves are literally studies in disillusionment. The products of the imagination are demolished by reality and the rational view of things, and the dreamer, like the child in "Chickamauga," wakes to a living nightmare.

Because Bierce saw nothing in life to look forward to, he spent much of it looking backward.[7] His truest art is the result of his nostalgia, which he objectifies as some false assumption experience ruthlessly denies. Perhaps just because it had proved so insubstantial and unreliable in his own case, Bierce sometimes wrote about the imagination as if it were itself a "dream" he could never hold on to. Only in sleep and dreams did it have a valid existence, and so "the dreamer is your only true poet; he is 'of imagination all compact.'" But Bierce also held that "imagination is merely memory," and since a dream is "a loose and lawless collocation of memories," "a resurrection of the dead," [8] the acts of dreaming, imagining, and remembering blurred in Bierce's mind as a single experience, oriented about the most exciting and promising interlude of his life. These dreams—or memories—he wanted very much to turn into permanent literature.

> I hold the belief that the Gift of Dreams is a valuable literary endowment—that if by some art not now understood the elusive fancies that it supplies could be caught and fixed and made to serve we should have a literature "exceeding fair." [9]

It was in a tone of regret that Bierce confessed: "I have no salt to put upon the tail of a dream's elusive spirit." [10]

In view of his emphasis upon the primacy of imagination, it is hardly surprising that next to poetry, Bierce regarded the romance as the noblest literary form. It was, in fact, the only type of fiction that Bierce would allow, the only kind that could be dignified with the name of "art." In using the term "romance," Bierce had in mind the same sort of distinction Hawthorne makes in his prefaces to *The Marble Faun* and to *The House of the Seven Gables;* that is, that whereas the novel follows closely the events of everyday life, the romance, far less bound to actuality, treats situations removed from ordinary life and experience. The principal difference, as Hawthorne expressed it, was between the novelist's "very minute fidelity" "to the probable and ordinary course of man's experience," and the romancer's "latitude" in presenting his truths "of the human heart" "under circumstances . . . of the writer's own choosing or creation." [11] By the time Bierce was writing, this basic distinction of modes had, of course, become the major controversy over literary realism, the avowed purpose of which was a "very minute fidelity" "to the probable and ordinary course of man's experience."

Led by Howells' influence and circumstances of material prosperity and social awareness, literary realism progressed steadily until its products were rivaled in popularity only by the sentimental and historical novel. The romance as Bierce conceived of it had either gone underground or degenerated into an ersatz form characterized by a strong love interest, extravagant adventure, and the inviolable formula of the happy ending. But the true romance had its able defenders, and Bierce was by no means alone in opposing a type of fiction he defined in *The Devil's Dictionary* as "the art of depicting nature as it is seen by toads," "a story written by a measuring-worm." [12] In fact, he had a perhaps unrecognized ally in the person of Frank Norris. Norris' lucid "plea for romantic fiction" is instructive both for its vigorous defense of the romance and for its attempt to distinguish between the romance and sentimental or historical novels at a time when these terms were being used interchangeably. Calling romance "the kind of fiction that takes cognizance of variations from the type of normal life," realism "the kind of fiction that confines itself to the type of normal life," [13] Norris goes on to state one of the main arguments against literary realism:

> The reason why one claims so much for Romance, and quarrels so pointedly with Realism, is that Realism stultifies itself. It notes only the surface of things. For it, Beauty is not even skin deep, but only a geometrical plane, without dimensions and depths, a mere outside.[14]

Norris' definition of the romance is even closer to Bierce's position. The romance, Norris claims, is "an instrument, keen, finely tempered, flawless," which could cut "down deep into the red, living heart of things." [15] Its principal merit, however, was its great freedom of conception and treatment:

> But to Romance belongs the wide world for range, and the unplumbed depths of the human heart, and the mystery of sex, and the problems of life, and the black, unsearched penetralia of the soul of man.[16]

Bierce was even more extravagant in extolling the endless possibilities of the romance. Of the romanticist he writes:

> The vitality of his art is eternal; it is perpetually young.

> He taps the great permanent mother-lode of human interest. His materials are infinite in abundance and cosmic in distribution. Nothing that can be known, or thought, or felt, or dreamed, but is available if he can manage it. He is lord of two worlds and may select his characters from both. In the altitudes where his imagination waves her joyous wing there are no bars for her to beat her breast against; the universe is hers . . . she may do as she will.[17]

While Bierce's love of the romance stemmed from his own temperament and deepest needs, he was not an isolated figure standing against a swelling flood of realistic fiction or historical novels. He took no active role in the literary controversy being conducted in the leading magazines, but he was generally as aware as Norris was of the basic issues involved. Moreover, his unequivocal stand in favor of the romance is a point frequently overlooked by those who have written about Bierce's short stories.

Because he held literature in such high regard, Bierce found its contemporary practice a dismal spectacle, and his list of literary offenders is a long one. In addition to realism, it includes local color, slang, dialect, historical novels, the happy ending, and fiction with a purpose—whether religious, sociological, or nationalistic. In fact, his exclusions pretty well eliminated the prevailing genres and practices of his time. His dislike of realism was made still more extreme by the fact that he did not care for the novel per se, although in referring to it he almost always meant the realistic novel. Bierce did not deny that great novels had been written, but they were the work of "great writers" who "had 'laid waste their powers' to write them." [18] In assimilating the new techniques of realism, the novel, Bierce maintained, had doomed itself to eventual oblivion. Furthermore, Bierce accepted Poe's theory of the single impression, and thus shared his belief in the superiority of the short story which could concentrate its effects. The novel, on the other hand, was a "diluted story—a story cumbered with trivialities and nonessentials." [19] He defines the form as:

A short story padded. A species of composition bearing the same relation to literature that the panorama bears to art. As it is too long to be read at a sitting the impressions made by its successive parts are successively effaced, as in a panorama. Unity, totality of effect, is impossible; for besides the few pages last read all that is carried in mind is the mere plot of what has gone before. [20]

Bierce's most significant statements, however, are those contrasting the severe limitations of the realistic novel with the "free wing of the romancer."

To the romance the novel is what photography is to painting. Its distinguishing principle, probability, corresponds to the literal actuality of the photograph and puts it distinctly into the category of reporting; whereas the free wing of the romancer enables him to mount such altitudes of imagination as he may be fitted to attain; and the first three essentials of the literary art are imagination, imagination and imagination.[21]

The realistic novel was "the lowest form of imagination" because it was "imagination chained to the perch of probability." [22] It had its principal champion in Howells, Bierce felt, because Howells was "destitute of that supreme and almost sufficient literary endowment, imagination." [23] Consequently, Bierce saw Howells' literary criticism as an elaborate defense growing out of his own limitations as an artist. Of course, Bierce objected to Howells on several other grounds, including Howells' beliefs that fiction should be democratic in its appeal, that it should deal largely "with the more smiling aspects of life," and that it should never disdain "the office of teacher." [24] But as far as Bierce's own aesthetic is concerned, the most important aspect of his attack is his fundamental distinction between realism's adherence to probability and the romance's inherent freedom from the prosaic and actual. To what extent Bierce was able to rid himself of the prosaic and actual, or what methods he employed to do so, are matters for subsequent consideration. The exact kind of literature he *wanted* to write sheds light on his actual performance.

If the realistic novel was "chained to the perch of probability," the romance was "fiction that owes no allegiance to the God of Things as They Are." [25]

In the novel the writer's thought is tethered to probability, as a domestic horse to the hitching-post, but in romance it ranges at will over the entire region of the imagination—free, lawless, immune to bit and rein.[26]

When the novel begins to violate probability, "another name for the commonplace," [27] it moves in the direction of the romance which is "essential and permanent." [28] The romance, in fact, may even deal with the "impossible," provided only that "what is related *seem* probable in the reading—*seem* true." [29] Thus Bierce says of the genuinely talented storyteller:

Suppose he relates the impossible; what then? Why, he has but passed over the line into the realm of romance, the kingdom of Scott, Defoe, Hawthorne, Beckford, and the author of the *Arabian Nights*—the land of the poets, the home of all that is good and lasting in the literature of the imagination.[30]

Opposed to such "masters in the House of Life" are the "little fellows," the "so-called realists." Bierce wonders if this lesser breed

ever think of the goodly company which they deny themselves by confining themselves to their clumsy feet and pursuing their stupid noses through the barren hinterland, while just beyond the Delectable Mountains lies in light the Valley of Dreams, with its tall immortals, poppy-crowned? [31]

Unfortunately, Bierce's remarks on the romance create more heat than light. His belief in the romance's superiority is perfectly clear, and so is his understanding of what the form *is*, and how it differs from realistic fiction. What is not clear, however, is what the romance *does*. Bierce has little to say about what goes on once the writer crosses "over the line into the realm of romance," "the land of the poets." The closest he comes to this problem is to tell us that the romanticist "can represent life, not as it is, but as it might be; character, not as he finds it, but as he wants it." But Bierce never suggests what governing conceptions, if any, determine the kinds of choice the romancer can make. He tells us that "men of sane judgment and taste still illuminate their minds and warm their hearts in Scott's suffusing glow"; that "the strange, heatless glimmer of Hawthorne fascinates more and more." [32] The question is *why?*

In lumping together Scott and Hawthorne, Defoe

and Beckford, writers whose approach to romance is hardly the same, Bierce makes us wonder if perhaps he loved the romance largely as a means of escape through fantasy, or through identification with situations far removed from real life. As a sort of "legitimate" flight from reality, the romance has a logical appeal since it enables the reader to live imaginatively in a realm where all things are possible, where life is "as it might be," character "as he wants it." The extravagant terms Bierce uses in praising the romance imply that his attitude was more emotional than critical. It is worth noting, for example, that Bierce locates the realm of imagination beyond the "Delectable Mountains" in the "Valley of Dreams"; its geography is strikingly similar to that of his fondest memories of his war days and of youth's hopeful dreams. As we have already seen, Bierce responds most to the romance's freedom to create fictive realities radically different from one's actual circumstances; nowhere does he consider the romance as a means of defining reality by distorting it, or of using it, as Hawthorne did, to sound the truths of the human heart and thus relate himself as artist to the "magnetic chain of humanity." To Bierce, the less fiction had to do with facts, the better: "Narrative fiction, intended as fiction, should seldom be based upon actual occurrences. Facts interfere with imagination, and imagination surpasses fact, and is the truer." [33] In his own short stories, the "facts" are always interfering with the "imagination." A world of destructive actuality annihilates the realm of romance and dreams. Bierce's despair was his realization that it was the fact, and *not* the imagination, that was the "truer."

Bierce's attitude toward science, for example, is curiously ambivalent. Sometimes he writes as if he admired science's detached and disinterested contemplation of things as they are. In the midst of a mad world "stands Science, inaccessible to its malign influence and unaffectable [sic] by the tumult. Why?—how? God knows; I only perceive that the scientific mind has an imagination of its own kind." The scientist sees the inscrutable perfection of the universe and knows man's insignificance in the face of vast "cosmic conditions," yet he "is not impressed with 'the sadness of it,' feels no desperation—sees nothing in it. He keeps his head—which, by the way, is worth keeping." [34] At other times, however, Bierce looked upon science as the sinister enemy of the imagination, a destroyer, like reason, of beautiful illusions. In his essay "Poetry and Verse," Bierce laments the fact that "the world is nearly all discovered, mapped and described," and that only in remote areas "Fancy waves her joyous wing unclipped by knowledge." [35]

As in the material world, so in the world of mind. The daring incursions of conjecture have been followed and discredited by the encroachments of science, whereby the limits of the unknown have been narrowed to such mean dimensions that imagination has lost her free, exultant stride, and moves with mincing step and hesitating heart.[36]

It was not so, Bierce claims, in "the youth of the world" when there were "none of the disillusionizing [sic] sciences with which a critical age, delving curiously about the roots of things, has sapped the substructure of religion and art alike." [37] In arguing that the greatest art is produced by nonscientific societies and eras, Bierce is on rather shaky ground. What explains the specious reasoning, however, is his personal sense of conflict between emotional and rational responses to experience—a conflict that definitely "sapped the substructure" of his own art and made fiction impossible.

Unable to mediate between his head and his heart, between his rational self and his imaginative idealistic self, Bierce ended by exploiting the differences with a ruthless cynicism that reflected his frustration. As a writer he first distrusted, then tried to deny, his most creative impulses. He was always being pulled in opposite directions by his realistic satirical journalism and his romantic views on literature, by his antifactual imagination and his distrust of all that was not fact. He loved the romance because it was free from "the God of Things as They Are," yet he defined a cynic as "a blackguard whose faulty vision sees things as they are, not as they ought to be." He praised the artistic imagination as a supreme endowment, yet referred to it as "a warehouse of facts, with poet and liar in joint ownership." [38] Because he was trapped by his own polarities, he came to look on everything in terms of violent contrasts and opposites: those who were not friends must be enemies; the English were civilized, Americans were barbarians; if he was right, all others were automatically wrong. As dogmatism and cynicism grew with his disgust, serious fiction became impossible for there was nothing he could take seriously any more. Life became a bitter joke to which Bierce responded with the kind of laughter he defines in *The Devil's Dictionary*: "An interior convulsion, producing a distortion of the features and accompanied by inarticulate noises." [39]

The polarity which Bierce was most conscious of, and which best summarizes all the others, was that between the true and permanent art he hungered for and the largely ephemeral journalism which took up his time and energy for almost forty years. It is not a question of Bierce's newspaper work leaving little opportunity for fiction—many writers with equal or greater demands upon their time have produced more imaginative literature than he did. The real significance of his journalism is that it defines, just as it intensified, the split between Bierce's imaginative and his empirical responses to life, between his desire to create an imaginary world of beauty, order, and permanence and an even stronger impulse to destroy a painfully real civilian world of windy oratory and business chicanery, of cheap patriotism and crass materialism. Both his short stories and his expository writing sprang from the common source of his postwar disillusionment which gave force and substance to his newspaper work while at the same time it undermined his attempts at serious fiction. The antithesis he saw between the new literary realism and the romance is a further reflection of Bierce's divided sensibility, as are the war stories themselves. The stories do not try to solve the problem of the split; they cannot, because Bierce could not solve it in his own life. But they do recreate it dramatically, sometimes with astonishing success. It is when Bierce turns away from the war and all that it symbolizes of his deepest feelings that his fiction suffers or shrinks to a largely mechanical concern with the business of storytelling.

During the years when Bierce was writing the stories which appeared in book form in 1891 as *Tales of Soldiers and Civilians*, his fame as a West Coast journalist was at its height. No hypocrisy or fraud, no instance of mediocrity or political graft, was too small to escape the acidic bite of his pen. The extent of his reputation, in fact, was the reason that young Hearst, with his flair for showmanship and instinct for profit, hired Bierce in 1887 as the star attraction for his recently acquired San Francisco *Examiner*. Under Hearst's shrewd control, the *Examiner*'s circulation increased rapidly, and with it, the impact of Ambrose Bierce as journalism's most feared–and fearless–cynic and satirist. In a contemporary sketch of Hearst's paper, Allan Kelly, himself a reporter and later an editor on the *Examiner* staff, said of Bierce's writing: "The most noteworthy literary feature of the *Examiner* has been and still is the publication of the work of Ambrose Bierce." [40] Seen as part of the inevitable reaction against the crudities of the Gilded Age, there is nothing unique about Bierce's newspaper polemics. As one critic of the period has suggested:

> Whosoever looked clearly at the extravaganza of the Gilded Age, with its immitigable farces of Tweeds and Fisks, its orgies of preemption and bribery, all staged to an accompanying music of patriotism and moral piety, ended by becoming cynical at heart.[41]

If Bierce ended by becoming a cynic, perhaps the most famous this country has produced, he began as something quite different. Because he turned cynicism into a career and made a profession of his misanthropy, it is sometimes assumed that Bierce thrived on his journalism and derived a weird delight from the gaudy spectacle of his age. In a sense he did, but largely because nihilism and sardonic wit became the only public responses he was capable of. Unable to reconcile his most creative impulses with the ugliness and stupidity he saw on every side, he "chose to explore the possibilities of hate as a form of creative energy." [42]

Such a decision, however, was not made with any relish, for it ran counter to all that Bierce had once hoped to do with a literary career. In fact, a good deal of Bierce's disillusionment stemmed from a gnawing sense of his own artistic limitations, as well as from his revulsion at a culturally starved and morally sick America. This is why Bierce always stressed an irreconcilable distinction between journalism and literature and why he actually despised the career which in his own day brought him considerable recognition. In a letter to a young female "pupil" he wrote:

> You ask me of journalism. It is so low a thing that it *may* be legitimately used as a means of reform or a means of anything deemed worthy of accomplishing. It is not an art; art, except in the greatest moderation, is damaging to it. The man who can write well must not write as well as he can; the others may, of course.[43]

What journalism lacked for Bierce was the quality of imaginative vision he prized so highly. It dealt only with prosaic facts and was, therefore, like the new realism he ridiculed, "mere reporting." Bierce never lost the feeling that his journalism was hack work and he had his doubts about the wisdom of including even a fraction of his total output in the *Collected Works.* In a letter written just a few months before he disappeared he confessed:

> One who has written as much worthless stuff as I have should not criticize "pot-boilers." Most newspaper work is nothing else. I found that not more than one-tenth of my work was worth putting into covers. And I'm not altogether sure about some that I *did* put into covers.[44]

Reading over the journalism Bierce did include, one is inclined to agree with his own estimate. Much of it is pungent and well written, but its very topical nature, the faded issues and forgotten figures, many obscure in their own day, robs it of any permanent vitality. His main justification for putting what he did in the *Collected Works* was that he wished a truly representative selection. He had, he said, reached his "literary level long ago," and since it was "not a high one," he felt it would be dishonest to make "it seem higher than it is by republication of my best only."[45]

If Bierce considered journalism the lowest form of literary activity, he regarded poetry as the highest. Bierce never doubted

> that the greatest man is the man capable of doing the most exalted, the most lasting and most beneficial intellectual work—and the highest, ripest, richest fruit of the human intellect is indubitably great poetry. The great poet is the king of men; compared with him, any other man is a peasant; compared with his, any other man's work is a joke.[46]

This "ripest, richest, fruit of the human intellect" eluded Bierce all his life, and he was so conscious of the disparity between his idealization of the art and his actual performance in it that he wrote relatively little poetry. He wrote considerable satirical "verse," most of which he included in the *Collected Works*, but he always carefully distinguished it from true poetry. Bierce's friend, the editor Jerome Hart, tells of the time he told Bierce his poetry lacked emotional appeal. To this Bierce replied: "You're right . . . Hart, let me tell you something. When I was in my twenties, I concluded one day that I was not a poet. It was the bitterest moment of my life." [47] In his letters to George Sterling, whose poetry he greatly admired, Bierce often referred to his own frustrated efforts at poetry in a tone of wistful regret.

> When old Homer, Shakespeare and that crowd—building better than Ozymandias—say: "Look on my works, ye mighty, and despair!" I, considering myself specifically addressed, despair. The challenge of the wits does not alarm me.[48]

Another time he remarked: "I consider poetry the flower and fruit of speech and would rather write gloriously than sensibly. But if poets saw things as they are they would write no more poetry." [49]

Of course, there is something curiously naïve in Bierce's notion that great poets are possessed of a divine frenzy and that writing "gloriously" precludes their writing "sensibly" or seeing things as they are. The remark makes more sense if seen as a projection of his inability to mediate between his feelings and his intellect and as part of his fuzzily romantic concept of the imagination. With his penchant for rigid classifications and dichotomies, Bierce found his own imagination crippled since, as a satirical journalist he "saw things as they are," whereas the literature he revered was free of "the God of Things as They Are." Unable to write as "gloriously" as he would have liked, he felt that he could only write "sensibly"—that is, rationally, unemotionally, without imagination. He never seems to have considered that true art also comes from close observation and experience of things as they are; he saw it instead as a mysterious realm far removed from real life. And that is why he idealized it, just as he idealized his war memories and the past in general. At the same time that he looked back nostalgically at the period of youthful ideals and enthusiasms, he distrusted his imagination for playing him false, so that his attitude wavers between sentimentality and bitter derision of all sentiment and untested assumptions. He was never quite sure himself which side he was on; sometimes he resembles the narrator in "A Son of the Gods," disillusioned but poignantly conscious of his dream; at other times he resembles the commander in the same story, undeceived by emotional appeals, "not a sign of feeling in his face." In a letter to Sterling, Bierce once made a remark that indicates how closely intertwined were his war memories, his youthful idealism, and his beliefs about literature. Discussing the thrill he had felt as a boy reading the classical and romantic poets, he wondered if anyone "can say accurately just how much of his joy in Homer . . . is due to love of poetry and how much to a renewel of mental youth and young illusions." [50] Like the protagonists in some of his war tales, Bierce was trapped between a yearning for "young illusions" and an empirical knowledge that demolished all such products of the imagination.

Convinced of an impossible gulf between satirical personal journalism and imaginative literature, Bierce decided to make the most of his destined career. As he told George Sterling, Bierce had "a preference for being the first man in a village rather than the second man in Rome" [51] and came to regard himself primarily as a satirist whose trade was "abuse." As for his long association with journals whose policies he disagreed with and whose character he "loathed," he confessed that "possibly the easy nature of the service had something to do with it." [52] Although he knew that "as a journalist . . . I am unapproachable in my line," [53] the knowledge gave him no real satisfaction, and there is something finally pathetic in the collapse of his literary ambitions. Thanking Sterling for the poet's praise of his work, Bierce added: "Things of that kind from too partial friends point out to me with a disquieting significance what I ought to be; and the contrast with what I am hurts." [54] Much of the abuse in his journalism comes from a well-established tradition of Western journalism, but with Bierce, a good deal of it arose from personal frustrations and limitations he could never really accept. When the California novelist Gertrude Atherton complimented Bierce on his writing, he told her:

> No, I'm not a great man. No one is better fitted to judge of greatness in men than I am, and I know that I am not great. I'm a journalist, past middle-age, without ambition, and have written nothing that measures up to my ideals.[55]

Although there is a hint of self-pity and self-dramatization in his remarks, Bierce was genuinely disturbed about not measuring up to his standards of excellence. Because he felt that he had failed to do anything permanently valuable in literature, Bierce devoted considerable time in his later years to encouraging impressionable young women in their literary aspirations and to perfecting the talent of other writers like George Sterling and Herman Scheffauer. His reason for doing this is significant since it reveals how concerned Bierce was with the problem of reputation —with establishing some lasting identity with art. As his friend Walter Neale has suggested, Bierce played the role of mentor to younger writers partly because it enabled him to display his erudition and air his opinions without fear of contradiction, but principally because he believed that these "disciples" would help insure his own immortality as a writer.[56] On the latter motive Bierce himself was equally explicit. He told Sterling: " I know that I have greater satisfaction in my slight connection with your . . . work than in my own. Also a better claim to the attention and consideration of my fellow-men." [57] In another letter to Sterling he said of him and Scheffauer: "It is through you two that I expect my best fame." [58] When one of his female disciples told the master she was abandoning the muse for marriage, Bierce generously forgave her: "You see, I expected that, as my pupil, you would bring me great glory (like George Sterling and some others) but if you are a good wife and mother I'll not complain." [59] Like many of his hopes and plans, Bierce's scheme to achieve fame as an artist at one remove, as it were, never worked out, partly because he insisted that his pupils accept his views without question, mainly because he never picked a first-rate talent to work with.

Bierce's sense of failure and defeat stemmed as much from discouragement over his age as over himself, for no one saw more clearly that the times were singularly unpropitious for his particular talents and imaginative vision. His considerable reputation as a journalist was mainly regional, confined to the West Coast and especially the San Francisco Bay region. There he *was* "the first man in a village." But Bierce lived and wrote well beyond the Western vogue of a boisterous and vituperative journalism, so that his later newspaper work, lacking the high spirits and ingenious insults of the tradition, seems heavy-handed and wooden. Moreover, by the time he received a more national exposure through his work for Hearst's newspapers and magazines, he had ceased to care about his career and was beginning to assemble material for the *Collected Works*. Having a low regard for journalism anyway, Bierce tried to dignify the practice of it by writing satire in the manner of Swift and Pope. He apparently felt that if he could not be a success as a poet or short story writer, he would settle for being a wit and would try to develop himself in a genre which had an honorable and well-defined history. In an essay called "The Passing of Satire," Bierce takes up the problem of satire in America by way of an imaginary dialogue between two figures known as the Melancholy Author and the Timorous Reporter. The Melancholy Author tells the Timorous Reporter:

"Satire cannot co-exist with so foolish sentiments as 'the brotherhood of man,' 'the trusteeship of wealth,' moral irresponsibility, tolerance, Socialism and the rest of it. Who can 'lash the rascals naked through the world' in an age that holds crime to be a disease, and converts the prison into a sanitarium?" [60]

What disturbs the Melancholy Author is that satire not only fails to reform, but even goes unappreciated as literature.

"Satire," said the Melancholy Author, "is punishment. As such it has fallen into public disfavor through disbelief in its justice and efficacy. So the rascals go unlashed. Instead of ridicule we have solemn reprobation; for wit we have 'humor'. . . . Why, sir, the American reading public hardly knows that there ever was a distinctive kind of writing known, technically, as satire—that it was once not only a glory to literature but . . . a terror to all manner of civic and personal unworth. If we had to-day . . . a Jonathan Swift or an Alexander Pope, he would indubitably be put into a comfortable prison with all sanitary advantages, fed upon yellow-legged pullets and ensainted by the Little Brothers of the Bad." [61]

Describing him as "intellectually the most homeless man of our time," Wilson Follett saw Bierce without any "sharply defined causes or goals to which he could give his allegiance (with the notable exception of a hatred of vice and folly), so that he vents his spleen on petty foibles and petty people." [62] But it was the pettiness of the age which disturbed Bierce most of all.

As indicated in the preface to the first edition of *Tales of Soldiers and Civilians*, Bierce found the door even more tightly closed against his fiction. Rejecting realism with its dreary detailing of actuality, hating the sentimental and historical novel, refusing to supply a happy ending "so long as stealing is more honorable and interesting," [63] Bierce found a large audience for his fiction hard to come by, although the reviews of his *Tales* were generally enthusiastic. It was actually the war stories that frightened off editors always ready to defer to their female readers; they found them too graphic, too grimly fatalistic, too out of step with the current sentimental treatment of the Civil War. As one anonymous British writer put it in reviewing the first English edition of *Tales:* "We should consider this part of the book [Civil War stories] extremely unsuitable for young readers, to whom it is surely more wholesome to present the nobler side of war." [64] Henry Canby once pointed out that the obvious cure for the falsifications and sugary distortions of reality in sentimental literature is "more truth." The honest writer "can be honest; but if he is much more honest than his readers, they will not read him." [65] What the public seemed to want was either a literature that dealt with "issues" realistically and in terms of some program of reform or else a literature that allowed them to escape unpleasant realities altogether. Bierce's war stories, at least, allowed the public to do neither. In a poem titled "Genius," a word Bierce defines as the "insight commercial" which knows what the public wants and gives it to them, he obviously was thinking of his own case when he wrote:

Lo! the lean rhapsodist whose soul surveys,
  Ecstatic, his unprofitable vision,
Interprets it in cleanly speech; arrays
  His jeweled words with scholarly precision!

Faith, he's a dunce or he would never lack
The means to wedge his belly from his back.[66]

Bierce's feeling of alienation from his age is certainly not unique in American literature. Serious American writers have a tradition of being at odds with their culture. What made Bierce's situation somewhat different, however, was that as a practicing journalist he was thrown into daily contact with the things which most irritated him—constantly tilting against graft, jingoism, nauseating sentiment, and all the crude tastes of a generally crude and materialistic age. It is not surprising that as he grew older and found himself increasingly isolated misanthropy gave way to indiscriminate hatred or that cynicism became not so much a reasoned philosophy of despair as a conditioned reflex, an instinctive lashing out at all that crossed his path. Nor is it strange that the split widened between his icy dissection of the real world's ugliness and his nostalgic yearning for a golden age of bright promise and noble achievement.[67] He came to resemble the protagonist in his story "A Resumed Identity" who watches a ghostly army pass by in the moonlight and searches in vain for his own outfit, only to discover that the war had ended years before and that his life "had spanned another life." [68] "The man looked curiously about him on all sides, as one who among familiar surroundings is unable to determine his exact place and part in the scheme of things."

Chapter IV

THE FAILURE OF THE NONMILITARY FICTION

ALTHOUGH Bierce's reputation as a writer of short stories rests largely on the war stories in *Tales of Soldiers and Civilians* (subsequently retitled *In the Midst of Life*), these constitute only a fraction of his fiction. In addition to the nonmilitary stories in the above collection and the twenty-four titles included in *Can Such Things Be?*, Bierce wrote over thirty-five stories and sketches. These are found in the *Collected Works* under such headings as "Negligible Tales," "The Parenticide Club," "The Way of Ghosts," "Some Haunted Houses," and "Mysterious Disappearances." With the exception of the appropriately named "Negligible Tales" and the stories of "The Parenticide Club," virtually all of Bierce's nonmilitary fiction deals in various ways with themes of terror and the supernatural. While a few of these stories are well done, none of them equal the best of Bierce's war tales, and several are almost unreadable. In all of them, in fact, there is a discernible reduction in imaginative power and control that indicates the extent to which Bierce's achievement in the war stories depended upon his own complex attitudes and the symbolic actions and images they educed in his mind. Before examining Bierce's work in the more conventional vein of terror and the supernatural, and its relationship to his war fiction, it is worth noting some stories which are in a quite different mode, the four outrageous tales of "The Parenticide Club."

In each of these stories, the worst that Bierce ever wrote, a psychopathic narrator describes the ingenious methods he employed to rid himself of parents or close relatives. What makes these phantasies so awful is not the atrocious crimes they portray, but their pointless sadism. Although Bierce apparently intended them to be wildy satirical, they make their strongest impression through the crazed narrator's delight in human suffering, which he details with undisguised relish. For example, in "My Favorite Murder," [1] the narrator, on trial for murdering his parents "under circumstances of singular atrocity," describes the still more heinous means by which he dispatched a hated uncle. Thus he is able to prove the "comparative triviality" of the first offense, and gains acquittal. The story itself is a "transcript" of his testimony. After the narrator has knocked his uncle senseless and "cut his hamstrings," he crams him into a sack which he then suspends a few feet off the ground by means of a rope tied to a nearby tree:

> Having completed my preparations, I imparted to the avuncular pendulum a gentle oscillation, and retiring to cover behind a contiguous rock, lifted up my voice in a long rasping cry whose diminishing final note was drowned in a noise like that of a swearing cat, which emanated from the sack.

The murder is then performed by a savage ram which

slowly reduces the uncle to "pulp" by charging the sack from distances up to a "quarter of a mile."

The entire account is neither amusing nor horrifying. It is simply in bad taste, and reflects an adolescent streak in Bierce that mars even some of his best stories. When the uncle is hit with particular force, the narrator tells us he "greatly enjoyed" the "superior quality of screams," or that he watched the ram's charge "with unspeakable pleasure." In fact, the only rationale for the story would seem to be expressed in the narrator's final remark: "Altogether, I can not help thinking that in point of artistic atrocity my murder of Uncle William has seldom been excelled." But it is the story itself, not the murder, that is the artistic atrocity. In "The Hypnotist," [2] an equally savage and pointless tale, the narrator uses his hypnotic powers to destroy his parents by telling them they are "wild stallions," bent on killing each other. This they proceed to do while their son watches contentedly.

> They plunged and reared backward upon their knees, struck savagely at each other with awkward descending blows of both fists at once, and dropped again upon their hands as if unable to maintain the upright position of the body. . . . Wild, inarticulate screams of rage attested the delivery of the blows; groans, grunts and gasps their receipt.

When the spectacle is over, "two battered, tattered, bloody and fragmentary vestiges of mortality attested the solemn fact that the author of the strife was an orphan." And that is all there is—senseless suffering and senseless brutality.

As stories, these morbid flippancies are worthless,

but they do show us something besides the fact that Bierce was capable of drivel. In their preoccupation with death and suffering they are further examples of the dominant theme in Bierce's fiction. The principal difference, of course, is that now he tries to turn this theme into a monstrous joke, as if he were trying to come to terms with death and suffering by reducing them to things laughable or ridiculous. Yet in his war stories, as we have already seen, there is never any laughter or ridicule over such matters. Furthermore, those who were closest to Bierce testify to his great sensitivity and to his disgust with all forms of pain and cruelty. The crude tales of "The Parenticide Club" are really symptomatic of the disastrous split between Bierce the cynical realist and Bierce the sensitive romantic and disillusioned idealist. Here, however, the latter Bierce has been effectively subdued by the bitter misanthrope, and Bierce's central fictional concern is so completely drained of all feeling and seriousness that the narrator turns into a pathological case, reveling in murder and mayhem. It is not that Bierce himself is abnormal, but since he has chosen to treat his subject without a trace of pity or concern, he must have a lunatic to relate these tales "full of sound and fury, signifying nothing." If Bierce was trying to write these sketches in the manner of Swift's "A Modest Proposal," his efforts fail, mainly because his violent sadism lacks the social and moral context upon which Swift's irony depends. This is precisely why they are so pointless and never go beyond the sadism they portray.[3]

The particular themes that Bierce treats in his fiction

are the kind that require the greatest delicacy and tact, so that his success as a writer of short stories depends heavily upon the management of tone. A story like "The Coup de Grâce" illustrates the tenuous line that divides the genuinely moving and pathetic from the sensational and revolting. Sergeant Halcrow's terrible agony is more horrible than anything in "The Parenticide Club," yet the story is made both moving and significant by the deep compassion of his friend Captain Madwell, and by the dignified way Bierce handles both men's ordeals in the "haunted forest." Since one of Bierce's main insights is that death itself is always "repulsive" and obscene, without dignity or meaning, whatever value the story is to have in human terms lies with the narrator's point of view. His attitudes are made still more important by the fact that under the conditions of Bierce's ironic and fatalistic vision, the characters themselves are essentially passive. They are victims rather than moral agents. Their hopes and dreams are proved false, and when they are brought face to face with "things as they are," life becomes unbearable. Thus the entire structure of Bierce's fictional world is under tremendous pressure, threatening to break down and turn his despairing insights into cynicism and sardonic humor.

Bierce believed, along with Walpole, that "life is a farce to him who thinks, a tragedy to him who feels." [4] His career as a writer of serious fiction ended when he could only see the human situation as a farce, since such a point of view removed the last trace of dignity from his characters. Instead of pathetic victims they became dupes, done in, not by the "pitiless perfection of the divine, eternal plan," but by Bierce's own mirthless laughter and mockery. Like the child in "Chickamauga" before his little world was swung around, Bierce looked upon human misery and decided that it must be a "a merry spectacle." The end result of this attempt to control his own feelings by denying them are the stories of "The Parenticide Club," or the kind of sophomoric statement we find him making in one of his unsuccessful ghost stories: "The most attractive object in the world is the face we instinctively cover with a cloth. When it becomes still more attractive—fascinating—we put seven feet of earth above it." [5] Most of this macabre humor is found in Bierce's journalism and scattered throughout *The Devil's Dictionary*. Although Bierce saw an impossible gulf between literature and life, the irony of his war stories is closely related to the realistic satire he wrote as a newspaperman. As Edwin Honig points out in his study of allegory:

> Irony is the traditional mode of the satirist hunting down the disparities which are understood to exist between man's moral and physical natures, between all sanguine expressions of hope in social ideals and in benevolent intentions and the unregenerate condition of actuality.[6]

When Bierce fails to maintain a consistent tone and point of view in his stories, it is usually because the satirical starts to override the ironic or serious; the tragedy threatens to turn into a farce.

In view of Bierce's sharply limited conceptions in the war stories, and the rigid and recurrent pattern that dramatizes them, it is hardly surprising that his best fiction comprises only about fifteen stories. After all, there is a limit to the fictional capital that can be made from the collapse of one's hopes and dreams. Bierce's war tales are idiosyncratic insofar as they show his preoccupation with a rational knowledge which undermines all sanguine assumptions and young illusions and invariably discovers life to be without meaning. This single insight is documented in story after story, but by its very nature it is self-limiting since it precludes the creation of any permanent values or transcendent meanings. Life becomes a series of contracting circles that stop only when the trap springs shut. Death simply points up the futility of it all.

> Done with the work of breathing; done
> With all the world; the mad race run
> Through to the end; the golden goal
> Attained and found to be a hole! [7]

And this, finally, is all that Bierce can tell us in his short stories.

Having created a world of the living that had no meaning, Bierce tried, in his tales of ghosts and the supernatural, to examine what lay beyond the grave. What he found was even more dismal and depressing than anything in life; it was the nightmare made permanent. Bierce's apparitions seldom speak at all, but in one tale, "The Moonlit Road," [8] the ghost of a strangled wife does tell the living what it is like in the "Realm of Terror." Speaking through the agency of "the Medium Bayrolles," the wraith describes how the dead "skulk in eternal dusk among the scenes of our former lives . . . hiding forlorn in lonely places; yearning for speech with our loved ones, yet dumb, and as fearful of them as they of us." But the real horror is that death brings no new knowledge or hope.

> You think that we are of another world. No, we have knowledge of no world but yours, though for us it holds no sunlight, no warmth, no music, no laughter, no song of birds, nor any companionship. O God! what a thing it is to be a ghost, cowering and shivering in an altered world, a prey to apprehension and despair!

While Bierce is not particularly concerned with the mental condition of ghosts, it is interesting to see how he imagines their psychology in terms of the same fear and isolation experienced by his protagonists in the war stories. Life-in-death only intensifies the death-in-life; both are realms of terror.

While an author's choice of subject is rarely an entirely conscious one, Bierce's ghost stories represent, in part at least, a deliberate attempt to find a wider audience and a better financial return from his fiction. In his excellent book *San Francisco's Literary Frontier*, Franklin Walker devotes a chapter to the great popularity, among California readers, of ghosts and the supernatural. "Western readers," he informs us, "have always called for horror yarns full of brutality and gruesomeness." [9] One has only to leaf through old volumes of a magazine like Bret Harte's *Overland Monthly* to confirm Walker's findings. It was in this magazine, in fact, that Ambrose Bierce's first story, "The Haunted Valley," [10] was published in 1871, but Bierce's tale is only one of many which deal in some way with themes of the bizarre and supernatural. Jerome Hart, for many years editor of the *Argonaut* and himself a lover of the *outré*, writes fondly of the tales that appeared in the pages of his newspaper. The titles that Hart mentions give us a good idea of the kind of fiction West Coast readers were looking for. In addition to the popular horror stories of W. C. Morrow and the pseudoscientific fiction of Robert Duncan Milne, Hart lists, among others, these suggestive titles: "Are the Dead Dead?" "A Warning Ghost" (Emma F. Dawson), "Occult Marriage" (Ella Cummins), "Metempsychosis," "The Withered Hand" (Annie Lake Townsend), "Ghoul's Quest" (Dan O'Connell).[11] As a California journalist and editor, Bierce encountered this type of fiction every day, and his own practice of it is very much in the tradition.

Bierce's tales of terror and the supernatural derive from his love of the romance and from his belief that literature must treat themes and situations far removed from everyday life. Because he looked upon it as a distant dream and the most memorable period of his life, the Civil War provided the desired diversion from a dreary world. When he had exhausted its possibilities in a few tales, he naturally looked for inspiration in what he calls in one of his stories "the realm of the unreal." In the words he uses to describe the artist's imagination, he would deal "with demons of the pit, with graves that yawn in pathways leading to light, with existences not of earth, both malign and benign—ministers of grace and ministers of doom." His interest in the supernatural is only another manifestation of a romantic temperament, as well as of a mind that habitually looked upon the dark side of life.[12] He defended the realm of the unreal as vigorously as he did the romance:

Tales of the tragic and the supernatural are the earliest utterances in every literature. When the savage begins to talk he begins to tell wonder tales of death and mystery—of terror and the occult. Tapping, as they do, two of the three great mother-lodes of human interest, these tales are a constant phenomenon—the most permanent, because the most fascinating, element in letters. Great Scott! has the patrol never heard of *The Thousand and One Nights*, of *The Three Spaniards*, of Horace Walpole, of "Monk" Lewis, of DeQuincey, of Maturin, Ingemann, Blicker, Balzac, Hoffman, Fitz James O'Brien? [13]

The quotation above is taken from an essay written in 1909 in which Bierce discusses how impossible it is for a writer to escape the charge of "imitation," since he works in long-established traditions and genres. To an extent, the essay may be a *post hoc* defense of his numerous excursions into the supernatural. Specifically, Bierce did have his own fiction in mind, for critics were forever discussing his stories as imitations of Poe. Reading over this sort of criticism, one can sympathize with Bierce's irritation: Poe seems to be lurking behind every subsequent tale of the supernatural, just as Walpole stands behind Poe. As one writer has sanely observed:

If all criticism were as perfunctory and fatuous as the majority of statements made about Ambrose Bierce's work, its case would be desperate indeed. One name—Edgar Allan Poe—has been repeated *ad nauseum* . . . although Bierce's resemblance to Poe as a writer does not seem to be evident in any special degree.[14]

Bierce admired Poe greatly, and adhered closely to some of his beliefs and theories of literature, especially those dealing with the short story. But his tales of the supernatural differ considerably from those of Poe—enough so, in fact, that comparisons are as apt to mislead as to enlighten. Bierce, for example, never dwells, as does Poe, on the minutiae of death and putrefaction. Nor did he share Poe's fascination with a mind observing its own madness and disintegration, and while he sometimes describes situations similar to those in Poe, Bierce lacked Poe's ability to sustain an atmosphere of horror or dread. In Poe's most successful stories, which truly are not of Germany, but of the soul, the material world is a symbolic projection of the protagonist's lurid mental life. Bierce's tales of terror, on the other hand, almost never employ such a technique or equal Poe's concentrated effects. The real similarity between both writers is not in their subjects or methods, but in the cast of their mind and temperament. Both were "mental aristocrats" with a dislike of democracy and men *en masse;* both liked to dramatize themselves; both responded to a sense of conflict between their feelings and their rational thoughts. In short, they were sensitive and romantic and readily victimized by their disappointments and frustrations. Poe was certainly the more talented and original; Bierce's anger over comparisons between his work and that of Poe was due in part to the fact that Bierce usually came off second best. Their resemblance, however, was not the result of "literary influence." Bierce would have written as he did even if Poe had never existed.

On the other hand, it is true that many of Bierce's stories are imitative in the sense that they deal in a rather conventional way with commonplace motifs. These are the kind of stories which, except for Bierce's highly individualistic style, could have been done as well or better by a number of writers, and for this reason they are not discussed in detail in this study. Some of the more common motifs Bierce uses include: the avenging ghost ("The Middle Toe of the Right Foot"); the invisible presence ("The Damned Thing"); the foolish wager to stay alone with the dead ("A Watcher By the Dead"); a disaster communicated by telepathy ("A Psychological Shipwreck"); an heirloom haunted by the fate of its ancestral owner ("John Bartine's Watch"); the man who falls asleep and dreams of a horrible event that took place years before in the same spot ("The Secret of Macarger's Gulch"). As ghost stories, there is no reason to disparage these tales, but any acquaintance with the genre they represent shows that they treat the unusual in the usual way. The characters are the same cardboard figures we meet in the typical tale of the supernatural, they speak the same stilted aristocratic dialogue, have the same experiences with the unknown and terrifying. In *The Devil's Dictionary*, Bierce defines a ghost as "the outward and visible sign of an inward fear,"[15] but in a number of his stories, the outward and visible is all there is. The ghosts are simply there as external facts, and the stories, all trite surface, elaborate their effect upon the protagonist. They are clever and entertaining, but that is all. Bierce is much more frightening in some of his war stories. If Bierce's more conventional tales of the supernatural tell us anything, it is that he was often more interested in diversion than in using the genre for purposes of symbolic statement.

Unlike most of the stories in the later editions of *Can Such Things Be?*, "Haïta the Shepherd" [16] has nothing to do with the supernatural; in fact, it was included among the nonmilitary tales in the first 1891 edition of Bierce's fiction. The story, an ingenuously transparent allegory about the elusive nature of happiness, is not especially distinguished. Bierce's treatment is too openly didactic to sustain the familiar insight that happiness flees when consciously sought and appears only when least expected. In the story's very simplicity, however, lies its relevance, for "Haïta the Shepherd" presents in sharp outline the principal features of Bierce's fiction which we have already observed in the war stories. It is really an abstraction of the movement from naïve innocence to a rational understanding which precludes the possibility of happiness altogether. As the story opens, we are told: "In the heart of Haïta the illusions of youth had not been supplanted by those of age and experience." Living a life of natural piety "devoid of ambition," the shepherd boy at first appears idyllically happy as he tends his flocks or prays to the shepherd god Hastur. But Hastur is a jealous god and when he has been offended he sends violent storms which drive Haïta to the uplands and destroy the cities in the valleys far below. It is Haïta's sympathetic identification with these "poor souls" which starts him thinking about man's ultimate destiny and his own annihilation: "It was through thinking on these mysteries and marvels, and on that horrible change to silence and decay which he felt sure must some time come to him . . . that Haïta first became conscious how miserable and hopeless was his lot."

Haïta's happiness flees precisely when he begins to ponder the imponderables—to question the very grounds of his existence. In fact, philosophical speculation, which he is powerless to control, makes him miserable:

> Pondering these things Haïta became melancholy and morose. . . . In every breeze he heard whispers of malign deities whose existence he now first observed. Every cloud was a portent signifying disaster, and the darkness was full of terrors.

Significantly, such thoughts cause him to neglect his sheep. Instead of searching out new pasturage he takes them back to the same spot every day "through mere abstraction, while puzzling about life and death—of immortality he knew not." "Indulging in the gloomiest reflections," Haïta is incapable of any positive action, paralyzed by his new sense of life's apparent meaninglessness and his own insignificance. Just as happiness flees with thought, so does it appear miraculously when the shepherd resolves to "no longer be a suppliant for knowledge which the gods withhold." A beautiful maiden surrounded by dazzling light suddenly materializes before him and tells the enraptured boy she will stay with him as long as he is "truthful and dutiful." As soon as he asks her name, however, and why she has come, the apparition fades. The rational mind has destroyed the beautiful illusion and "the landscape was darkened by a giant shadow sweeping across the valley." Three times she comes and as often diasppears when questioned, leaving Haïta "forlorn."

Puzzled by his elusive vision, the shepherd goes for enlightenment to a "holy hermit" who asks the reason for his sorrow "that age may minister to the hurts of youth with such balms as it hath of its wisdom." But the wisdom of age can hardly allay "the hurts of youth"; all it can do is define the boy's destructive experience in the same kind of rational terms which brought it about:

> Know, then, that her name, which she would not even permit thee to inquire, is Happiness. Thou saidst the truth to her, that she is capricious for she imposeth conditions that man can not fulfill, and delinquency is punished by desertion. She cometh only when unsought, and will not be questioned. One manifestation of curiosity, one sign of doubt, one expression of misgiving and she is away!

As the wise old man of Bierce's little fable, the hermit has himself seen the maiden in his youth, but his blunt explication to Haïta suggests that such illusions no longer trouble his lonely existence. Like the commander's sinister reflections in "A Son of the Gods," the rational faculties seem to be the cause of man's unhappiness, yet the real, or final, cause lies outside man's control or responsibility, in the "pitiless perfection of the divine, eternal plan" or, to use the hermit's words, in "conditions that man can not fulfill." Thus, while the rational mind demolishes the lovely dream, it is preferred as experiential and mature wisdom, even though it impoverishes life. Similarly, the dream itself is ambiguous, hauntingly desirable and at the same time deceptive and "capricious." In the war essays an analogous situation exists: Bierce's war experience as a whole is drenched in a romantic light that never was and defined in the terms of some cherished dream he longs to recapture. The dream, however, rudely disappears whenever Bierce describes the repulsive look of a mutilated corpse or the death agony of a man whose brains protrude from his skull. As Bierce indicates in the final rhapsodic section of "What I Saw of Shiloh," he himself did not understand how he could hold such opposing points of view about the same experience. The nostalgic passages simply fail to harmonize with the naturalistic descriptions, although they seem to submerge them in the haze of romantic memory. In the war stories, on the other hand, the rational wisdom of age sees through the illusions of youth. As in "The Mocking-bird," the "Realm of Conjecture" demolishes the "Enchanted Land"—unintentionally, but unavoidably.

In his own life Bierce found happiness as elusive as Haïta discovers it to be. In the letters and essays he refers to it again and again as the only goal worth seeking, a somewhat unusual attitude considering his insight in "Haïta the Shepherd" and a number of other stories. It was as if he could never quite accept what his reason told him to be true, and so we find him insisting:

> The one purpose of every sane human being is to be happy. No one can have any other motive than that. There is no such thing as unselfishness. . . . We move on lines of least reluctance. Whatever tends to increase the beggarly sum of human happiness is worth having; nothing else has any value.[17]

He even brings the matter up in "To Train a Writer," where we saw his determination to deracinate the fledgling author and strip him of all ideals and illusions: "Happiness should disclose itself to his enlarging intelligence as the end and purpose of life; art and love as the only means to happiness." [18] Yet at the same time Bierce would have him know that the world is "false, cruel, cursed with illusions—frothing mad!" Bierce's career is dominated by this same precarious balance between emotional sensitivity and a rational distrust of his feelings—of emotion itself, that "prostrating disease caused by a determination of the heart to the head." [19]

From the standpoint of Bierce's over-all thematic concerns, "Haïta the Shepherd" touches on an issue far more important than the evanescent nature of happiness. Haïta's disturbing reflections on the human condition and the mystery of existence turn upon the single idea of death itself, "that horrible change to silence and decay which he felt must some time come to him." The thought of his own extinction transforms the very breeze into "whispers of malign deities" and fills the darkness with "terrors." When General Clavering tells Parker Adderson that "death is horrible," the would-be "philosopher" tries to dismiss its horror as an instance of atavism, part of man's nonrational heritage, but susceptible to the light of reason. The irony, of course, is that Adderson's spectacular collapse when he is faced with immediate death refutes the very point he had been making with such smug composure. Adderson becomes another victim of his own inadequacy, in this case a casualty of what Bierce calls elsewhere the "ancestral bond." He travels "not the mental road he would, but the one that he must," burdened with all kinds of unregenerate instincts and emotions he cannot control. What gives "Parker Adderson, Philosopher" its significance, however, is not the fact that its protagonist falls prey to atavistic terror (such a theme appears in Bierce's fiction with insistent regularity), but that the power of reason—that faculty of seeing things exactly as they are which Bierce so often insisted upon—can itself be an illusion. When this happens, the irrational emotion becomes more "real" than the rational explanation; "imagination surpasses fact, and is the truer," as Bierce once remarked of romance. Bierce realized that reason cannot cope with powerful instinctive emotion, especially terror; in fact, this is the rationale for his tales of ghosts and the supernatural. But he also insisted that reason could subdue the creative imagination, most often when the latter produces sanguine assumptions.

Such a two-sided conception suggests why Bierce could romanticize his own war memories, despite a full knowledge of war's horror and why, at the same time, the war stories present some horror of death or defeat which destroys whatever illusions or naïve hopes the protagonist may have had. It is interesting to note how his most romantic writing occurs in private correspondence or in personal essays which deal nostalgically with youthful experience. It is as if Bierce were insisting on the validity of his own dreams while denying everyone else theirs. As the satirist and cynic on public display, or the unflinching narrator of fictional disaster, Bierce exposes deception and crushes illusion with ruthless abandon; as the romantic dreamer of his private "enchanted forest," he finds reason as useless as Parker Adderson did. He distrusted his feelings, yet responded emotionally. He distrusted his rational faculties—and found their insights intolerable —yet persisted in reducing life to facts. Unable to integrate his conflicting attitudes, Bierce could only write stories which depict the hopeless struggle between rational knowledge and imaginative experience. The conflict destroys the protagonist just as it destroyed Bierce's career as a short story writer or his youthful ambition to be a poet. With defeat, the rational "fact" of the human condition as Bierce saw it, comes death, symbol of life's final inanity and of the paralysis that results (as it does to Haïta) from philosophical speculation. It is this compulsive preoccupation with death and all its implications that constitutes the "commanding center" of Bierce's fiction and unites his war stories with the tales of the supernatural. The thought of death and of his own nonbeing (in terms of artistic achievement and alienation from his age) had a powerful hold on Bierce's mind, as is evidenced by his incessant references to it in everything he wrote. When he submitted imaginatively to its force he could create a few profoundly disturbing excursions into the realm of horror and the supernatural. Too often, however, he ruined his effects with a smugly superior tone or a flippancy reminiscent of Parker Adderson. He tried to resist with his intellect and his cynicism the whole basis of the story, or else wobbled uncertainly between accepting and rejecting his own imaginative creation.

No such uncertainty of tone mars "A Tough Tussle." [20] Despite is unfortunate title and a somewhat contrived conclusion, the story is an effective study in sheer terror. Although "A Tough Tussle" is found in the later editions of *Can Such Things Be?*, it appeared originally, like "Haïta the Shepherd," in *Tales of Soldiers and Civilians*. It really should be considered as a war story, not only because of its setting, but because it makes its impact without recourse to the supernatural. Its ghost is "the outward and visible sign of an inward fear," the imaginary creation of Second Lieutenant Brainerd Byring alone "in the heart of a forest in western Virginia." Moreover, as a war story, "A Tough Tussle" repeats the familiar pattern of Bierce's war fiction as a whole: the forest setting, the initiatory experience, the young brave hero undone by circumstances and his own frailty, the final twist of irony. And like the best of these stories, its success depends, not upon any richness of conception, but upon the symbolic integrity of its actions and images. While its theme of the overwhelming fear of death immediately suggests "Haïta the Shepherd" or "Parker Adderson, Philosopher," its most significant qualities are those found in such stories as "The Mocking-bird" or "A Son of the Gods," where Bierce manages to bring his own deepest feelings under imaginative control and to give an inward state of mind an objective metaphorical vitality.

For the setting of "A Tough Tussle" Bierce returns again to the Cheat Mountain country he describes so lyrically in "On a Mountain." Although it is early in the war, Lieutenant Byring has already proved himself in such battles as Phillipi, Rich Mountain, and Greenbrier. Like Bierce himself, he had enlisted as a private, was promoted to first sergeant, and received his commission when his captain was killed. Byring's ordeal takes place at night during a lonely tour of picket duty. The fatal flaw which brings it about is a severe case of necrophobia, coupled with an abnormally acute imagination which finds the darkness filled "with all manner of unfamiliar shapes, menacing, uncanny, or merely grotesque." Because the passage describing this weakness has important affinities with Bierce's own dilemma as a writer, it deserves examination:

> The exhilaration of battle was agreeable to him, but the sight of the dead, with their clay faces, blank eyes and stiff bodies, which when not unnaturally shrunken were unnaturaly swollen, had always intolerably affected him. He felt toward them a kind of reasonless antipathy that was something more than the physical and spiritual repugnance common to us all. Doubtless this feeling was due to his unusually acute sensibilities—his keen sense of the beautiful, which these hideous things outraged. Whatever may have been the cause, he could not look upon a dead body without a loathing which had in it an element of resentment. What others have respected as the dignity of death had to him no existence—was altogether unthinkable. Death was a thing to be hated. It was not picturesque, it had no tender and solemn side—a dismal thing, hideous in all its manifestations and suggestions.

While Brainerd Byring obviously is not Ambrose Bierce, nor is the story meant to yield biographical data, the passage quoted above parallels closely Bierce's own contrasting responses in his war essays. Bierce also found the "exhilaration of battle" "agreeable to him," and responded fully to the "beautiful" and "picturesque" aspects of his experience. At the same time, like Byring, he seems to have been fascinated by the repulsiveness of death; it violated "his keen sense of the beautiful." Utterly without dignity, it was "a dismal thing, hideous in all its manifestations." In the story Bierce uses some of the same terms we find in his description of the burned corpses or of the first encounter with death in the Cheat Mountain when he and his companions raised the blankets from some dead soldiers. As he says of Byring's feelings, Bierce's own attitude appears to have gone beyond the ordinary "physical and spiritual repugnance." The number of precisely detailed descriptions of dead or mutilated bodies is one indication of this, and so are the slightly hysterical attempts at levity. Whether Bierce actually had a pathological obsession with death is uncertain, and finally unimportant. What he did have unmistakably were unusually acute sensibilities, easily "outraged."

After Byring has been on watch for a time, he becomes aware of the dim outlines of a human figure dappled with patches of shadow and moonlight: "It was almost before his face as he sat; he could have sworn that it had not before been there." Drawing his pistol, he approaches cautiously and, "looking down upon the face," he sees "that it was a dead body." "With a feeling of sickness and disgust" Byring resumes his seat and tries to control a swelling "sense of the supernatural—in which he did not at all believe." Like Parker Adderson, he tries to explain away his fear of death on the grounds of primitive inheritance. "What we inherit as a superstition our barbarous ancestors must have held as a reasonable conviction," he conjectures. They no doubt had their own reasons for regarding a dead body as "a malign thing endowed with some strange power of mischief." Although the belief in "the malevolence of the dead body" gradually faded from tradition, Byring is only too aware that "it left its heritage of terror, which is transmitted from generation to generation—is as much a part of us as are our blood and bones." Rousing himself from these reflections, he looks again at the corpse which now lies fully revealed in the moonlight. It wears the "uniform of a Confederate soldier."

The chest seemed unnaturally prominent, but the abdomen had sunk in, leaving a sharp projection at the line of the lower ribs. The arms were extended, the left knee was thrust upward. The whole posture impressed Byring as having been studied with a view to the horrible.

Byring would like to move, but he has arranged a rendezvous with his relief at this precise spot. Furthermore, his pride will not allow him to abandon his post —"he feared they would think he feared the corpse." "Unwilling to incur anybody's ridicule," Byring forces himself to look directly at the body.

As he stares at his "antagonist," death itself, his mind begins to disintegrate under the weight of his terror and he becomes obsessed with the conviction that the corpse has moved in the deceptive play of moonlight and shadow. "Crouching like a gladiator," "his whole body bathed in a chill perspiration," Byring can neither run nor "unfix his gaze from the face of the dead man." The longer he stares transfixed the more certain he is that "the horrible thing was visibly moving!"

When firing suddenly starts up along the picket line, the sound breaks "the spell of that enchanted man": "With a cry like that of some great bird pouncing upon its prey he sprang forward, hot-hearted for action!" The next morning the captain and surgeon from Byring's outfit, out looking for dead and wounded from last night's skirmish, find the lieutenant's body next to that of a Confederate private. The officer has a sword-thrust through his heart, but the private's body bears five "dreadful" gashes. Puzzled that there is only one weapon, Byring's sword, the surgeon turns curiously to the Confederate corpse:

> It was frightfully gashed and stabbed, but there was no blood. He took hold of the left foot and tried to straighten the leg. In the effort the body was displaced. The dead do no wish to be moved—it protested with a faint, sickening odor. Where it had lain were a few maggots, manifesting an imbecile activity.

Once again death and its terror claim their victim; what remains at the end is the meaninglessness of it all —the "faint, sickening odor," the "imbecile activity."

The success of "A Tough Tussle," like that of "A Son of the Gods," depends largely upon the narrator's precariously balanced point of view toward the experience he describes. This is more apparent in the latter tale where the narrator is himself a character witnessing the entire action. In "A Tough Tussle," Brainerd Byring's ordeal is related by the omniscient author; nevertheless, Bierce's own responses to his imaginative creation are just as functional in defining the meaning of the story and in enlarging its symbolic implications. Bierce takes up an ambiguous position midway between the two worlds he is contrasting: a daylight world of objective rational "facts" in which dead bodies stay dead and do not move and in which the supernatural can be logically explained, and a night-time world in which the dead appear to move and the darkness is filled with terrifying "shapes, menacing, uncanny, or merely grotesque." Because of his necrophobia and his "unusually acute sensibilities," Byring is unhinged and destroyed by "the sense of the supernatural—in which he did not at all believe." The entire story pivots on this contrast between the sense of the supernatural—its imaginative hold on the mind—and a rational view which registers its disbelief at the same time that it is being subverted. Such a situation is further defined by the narrator's ambiguous relationship to the deracinated officer. As the omniscient author standing outside the action, Bierce makes his denouement in the name of reason. But he also identifies himself closely with Byring and shares his intense discomfort. His sympathy is thus a measure of his assent to the power of the irrational. For example, he explains Byring's dilemma and its terrifying validity on the same grounds of heredity by which the lieutenant tries to rationalize his fears:

> I repeat that Lieutenant Byring was a brave and intelligent man. But what would you have? Shall a man cope, single-handed, with so monstrous an alliance as that of night and solitude and silence and the dead,—while an incalculable host of his own ancestors shriek into the ear of his spirit their coward counsel, sing their doleful death-songs in his heart, and disarm his very blood of all its iron? The odds are too great—courage was not made for so rough use as that.

The "odds" are always too great for a Bierce hero, whose courage is never equal to the test it is subjected to. This is the truly irrational horror, the "conditions that man can not fulfill."

All these ambiguities as to what constitutes reality—which is the knowledge and which is the dream—coalesce in the symbolic values Bierce assigns to his forest setting. As with a number of Bierce's tales, the central experience takes place in a densely wooded area which functions as a metaphor of some shocking insight into the inscrutable nature of existence. In fact, in "A Tough Tussle" Bierce carefully distinguishes his forest realm from the prosaic world of everyday life: "Ah, children of the sunlight and the gaslight, how little you know of the world in which you live!" Moreover, his descriptions of this strange borderland between appearance and reality identifies him still further with Byring's experience:

> He to whom the portentous conspiracy of night and solitude and silence in the heart of a great forest is not an unknown experience needs not to be told what another world it all is—how even the most commonplace and familiar objects take on another character.

It is the place where there "are translations in space of objects which have not been seen to move, movements wherein nothing is observed to change its place." Nothing is certain, everything has a peculiar duality which makes ambiguity the normative value. To Bierce the forest is the real world of fear and isolation, of unknown lurking antagonists and unknown possibilities of disaster. Characteristically, it is the world where anything strange may occur. Those who adhere to the "smiling aspects of life" never sense its existence, but Bierce lives in the very depths of his "enchanted forest." In his war essays it is a place of beauty and romantic possibility to which he longs to return; in his fiction it becomes a place of horror and defeat, for always, as its central enigma, death lies in wait and makes the universe "one primeval mystery of darkness, without form and void." Like Brainerd Byring, "that enchanted man," Bierce submits to the "spell," and becomes "the sole, dumb questioner of its eternal secret," his "keen sense of the beautiful" outraged by "these hideous things."

In the fullest symbolic sense, of course, Byring's "tough tussle" does not take place in a forest at all, but in the haunted solitude of his own mind. The struggle which destroys him is between two views of reality, the rational and the irrational, or the imaginative and the empirical. All of the actions and images of the story point to a man driven inward upon his imperfect mental resources, undone by a fatal imbalance which causes him to react in a manner contrary to what he knows he should believe and do. This imbalance, in turn, is signified by the ambiguous character of all experience in the forest and by Byring's uncertainty of response, the split between his disbelief in ghosts and his "sense of the supernatural." At the end of the story, these oppositions come together in a final chilling insight, just as the irrational becomes an empirical reality, explained in terms of the ancestral bond. The daytime world of objective fact and the light of reason is found to be just as awful and just as unacceptable in its way as the nighttime world of irrational terror. These worlds meet on the common ground of futility and mystery, for if man cannot resist the irrational element in his experience, neither can he explain what is signified by the maggots and their "imbecile activity." And that is the most shocking "fact" of all.

Although Bierce has frequently been praised for fertility of imagination, his imagination was actually restricted to a few conceptions which he repeats in story after story. To be sure, there is a certain mechanical ingenuity in the particular scenes and incidents he employs, but his fiction seldom varies in its larger strategies and design. Instead of developing imaginatively or intellectually, Bierce kept doubling back on his own tracks, artistically speaking, so that his plots and themes become tedious if taken in large doses. The basic similarity of his stories, including both the war tales and those dealing with terror or the supernatural, suggests that as a writer Bierce found himself as hopelessly trapped as any of his protagonists. He could never seem to break out of the charmed circle circumscribed by his vision of futility and inevitable defeat. Bierce may have read Darwin and Spencer along with other pessimists of the age, but he knew determinism at first hand, in his own warring impulses and inadequacies and in an environment which, to say the least, violated "his keen sense of the beautiful." The knowledge served only to feed his frustration and his resentment. While the over-all design of Bierce's stories is remarkably the same, their individual quality is not. From his outstanding achievement in a handful of stories, Bierce could descend to the worst kind of potboilers and adolescent nonsense. This wide fluctuation is most noticeable in the nonmilitary tales where Bierce had to manufacture his situations instead of drawing them from his immediate experience and his own complex feelings about the war. Generally speaking, the war tales have a uniform excellence that tells us much about the nature of Bierce's achievement as a short story writer.

In "The Man and the Snake" [21] we have a story so similar in conception to "A Tough Tussle," yet so inferior in artistic merit as to seem almost a caricature of the latter tale. It is "A Tough Tussle" without any of that story's suggestive ambiguities or symbolic vitality and compression. A comparison of the two stories shows what happened when Bierce failed to become seriously engaged in his own fictive creation or was unable to adopt any consistently relevant point of view toward his protagonist. In their basic outlines the stories are the same: the isolated "rational" protagonist, the unexpected encounter with a destructive stimulus, the mind cracking under the weight of irrational hereditary fear, death, the final ironic revelation. In "The Man and the Snake," the victim is a dilettante named Harker Brayton, "thirty-five, a scholar, idler and something of an athlete, rich, popular and of sound health." He is that very conventional figure, the wealthy bachelor with exotic tastes. As such, Brayton is difficult to respond to as a significant human being, and Bierce does not seem to find him very convincing either. "Stretched at his ease" as the story opens, Brayton has been reading an ancient account of the snake's ability to hypnotize its prey with its eyes. This, of course, Brayton regards with amused contempt: " 'The only marvel in the matter,' he said to himself, 'is that the wise and learned in Morryster's day should have believed such nonsense as is rejected by most of even the ignorant in ours.' " Brayton prides himself on being a "man of thought."

Brayton's encounter with the irrational takes place not in a lonely forest, but in the guest room of the eminent authority of snakes, Dr. Druring. The good doctor, who loves "nature's vulgarians" and refers to himself as the "Zola of zoölogy," keeps a large collection in his "Snakery." Although Brayton does not share Druring's "reptilian" "sympathies," he finds life at the mansion very pleasant—until he happens to glance under his bed while reading. There in the shadows he sees two beady eyes staring "into his own with a meaning, a malign significance." They belong to a large snake, coiled menacingly, which Brayton assumes to be an escaped specimen. Like Byring, he finds his situation "revolting" but hesitates to summon aid lest "the act might subject him to the suspicion of fear." At first he tries to retreat gracefully but discovers to his horror that he has moved forward instead. From this moment until his death from sheer terror, Brayton gives an involuntary demonstration of the ancient belief he had just been ridiculing. He is hypnotized by the snake's "pitiless malevolence" and his own irrational imagination. Apparently, the ancestral bond on this occasion has something to do with primitive snake worship, for as an entranced Brayton listens to savage music he believes himself standing "in the Nileside reeds hearing with exalted sense that immortal anthem through the silence of the centuries." All kinds of weird visions pass before him. In one, a huge snake wearing a crown looks at him "with his dead mother's eyes." What this signifies is never explained for Brayton suddenly falls flat on his face. Lifting his head, he "stared again into those baleful eyes and was again in bondage."

"Now," Bierce assures us, "ensued a fearful scene." Brayton wiggles, he squirms, he crawls on his belly like a reptile.

> There was froth upon his lips; it dropped off in flakes. Strong convulsions ran through his body, making almost serpentile undulations. He bent himself at the waist, shifting his legs from side to side. And every movement left him a little nearer to the snake. He thrust his hands forward to brace himself back, yet constantly advanced upon his elbows.

Meanwhile, back in the library, Dr. Druring is "in rare good humor," having just obtained an "*ophiophagus*" —"a snake that eats other snakes," as he explains to his wife. The conversation is suddenly interrupted by a piercing shriek from their guest upstairs, who is still human enough to register his fright. They find Brayton dead on his stomach, "his head and arms . . . partly concealed under the foot rail of the bed." The snake? "It was a stuffed snake; its eyes were two shoe buttons." Instead of a Brainerd Byring, unable to keep his eyes off a moonlit corpse, we have Harker Brayton, performing incredible contortions, mesmerized by a bogy under a bed. In "A Tough Tussle" the ending is both ironic and disturbingly significant. The daytime actuality of the stiffened, maggot-ridden corpse is more horrifying than its supposed animation, and the body itself defines both the rational human condition and the terror-haunted mind that perceives it. In "The Man and the Snake," on the other hand, all we have is the immobility—the trivial irony—of the taxidermist's art. "How did this thing get in here?" Druring asks as he sends it skidding across the floor. Its presence is merely ludicrous.

Bierce, however, was not trying to write a funny story. His purpose was to show how the power of suggestion can destroy a man as a rational being, and Bierce works hard at the spell it casts over Brayton. Yet there are examples of a labored facetiousness in "The Man and the Snake" typical of Bierce's least-successful fiction. The most damaging thing that can be said of them is that they serve no discernible purpose in the story. For example, almost one fifth of "The Man and the Snake" is devoted to irrelevant remarks about Druring's family or the architecture of the "Snakery," all presented in a clogged prose which strangles on its own verbosity.

> His wife and daughters, not having the advantage to share his enlightened curiosity regarding the works and ways of our ill-starred fellow-creatures, were with needless austerity excluded from what he called the Snakery and doomed to companionship with their own kind, though to soften the rigors of their lot he had permitted them out of his great wealth to outdo the reptiles in the gorgeousness of their surroundings and to shine with a superior splendor.

This remarkable sentence is from the man Edwin Markham praised, with justification, for the "crystal cleavage and clearness of his sentences." "Many of them end like rifle snaps. You don't know that you are struck until you see the blood spurt." [22]

The style Markham had in mind is the style encountered most often in the war stories where Bierce takes his characters seriously. Although his protagonists lack a complex psychology, they are convincing simply because Bierce believes in them. It is when he moves out of his haunted forest and into "the sunlight and the gaslight" that he begins to lose control over his tone and style. In effect, the internal split between reason and imagination, which he sometimes dramatizes so successfully, becomes a split between the story and its narrator. The result is a flawed technique marked by uncertainty of tone, a painful combination of humor and seriousness, and a breakdown in coherence and unity. Instead of the protagonist being pulled apart by things as they are, the story itself starts to unravel, a victim of Bierce's cynical disbelief in its significance or validity. The problem in "The Man and the Snake" is that Bierce cannot locate his sympathies—cannot get *inside* his protagonist—and neither can we. Brayton is about as stuffed and unreal as the specimen which scares him to death, and the whole story has a woodenness about it which makes amusement the most charitable response. In fact, Brayton, with his college education, his idle ways, and his smugly superior manner, is a type Bierce neither understood nor trusted, so that the story may have been subconsciously motivated by revenge.[23] Brayton is never mocked or sneered at, but there is a hint of sadistic pleasure in the description of his performance before the stuffed snake. In "A Tough Tussle" or "The Coup de Grâce," on the other hand, there is no mistaking the anguish of his soldier-victims or the sympathy it calls for.

In a curious story entitled "A Baby Tramp"[24] we have another example of Bierce's problem with tone and coherence in his nonmilitary fiction. The problem is even more apparent than in "The Man and the Snake." The protagonist is a little boy named "Jo Parlow," whose parents died in an epidemic that "carried away a full half of the population" of Blackburg when Jo was a year old. Three years later the ghost of Jo's mother is seen in the town cemetery by a group of May Day revelers on their way home from a neighboring festival. Since all the young people had known Hetty Parlow, there is no doubt about her being a ghost: "That established the thing's identity; its character as ghost was signified by all the customary signs —the shroud, the long, undone hair, the 'far-away look' —everything." While the revelers watch spellbound, Hetty Parlow's ghost is observed "stretching out its arms toward the west," calling the name of her son in an imploring voice. Jo, who has been adopted by distant relatives "on the opposite side of the continent," gets the message or, more accurately, feels a sudden inexplicable urge to travel. Although his progress is impeded by various misadventures, he moves inexorably eastward. For a while he is held captive by some "Piute Indians" who sell him to a woman "on one of the eastbound trains." He is even detained in the town of "Whiteville" and "sentenced to imprisonment in the Infants' Sheltering Home." Finally, however, he reaches Blackburg and the cemetery outside town. He is found dead upon his mother's grave.

"A Baby Tramp" is just the kind of story we might expect would give Bierce trouble. Its most interesting problem is not the plight of Jo Parlow, but that of the narrator who cannot seem to make up his mind whether the whole thing should be taken seriously or satirically. Furthermore, the story is filled with gratuitous information, and is told in a rambling, slipshod manner which suggests Bierce's uncertainty of purpose. For example, we are told that the "mysterious disease" which depopulated Blackburg was preceded by two other unusual events: a "shower of small frogs" and a "fall of crimson snow." This is followed by a long irrelevant account of Mrs. Parlow's family, the Brownons, their respectable position in the town, and the "young scapegrace named Parlow" whom Hetty married in Boston. The implication of all this is that Hetty married beneath her, but what bearing the fact might have on Jo's peregrinations is never revealed. It is as mysterious as the shower of small frogs. But it is Bierce's ambiguous attitude toward Jo himself that is most disconcerting. At first, it appears that satire is the intent. When the parents die, Bierce informs us, "at the age of one whole year Joseph set up as an orphan." In Cleveland, Ohio, a policeman notices him "deliberately toddling away" from the home of his most recent stepmother. Asked where he is going, Jo replies, "a doin' home." For a time Bierce seems to be conscious of a certain absurdity in the situation of a four-year-old "toddling" eastward, brooking no interference. Yet he also wants to see Jo as some sort of symbol of man's loneliness in an alien world. Because Bierce is unable to integrate his own feelings and conflicting points of view, the story vacillates between the pathetic and the ludicrous, although such ambiguity serves no purpose.

Near the end of "A Baby Tramp," Jo seems to be taken seriously when Bierce details his suffering, and by the time Jo reaches his destination, Bierce appears to find his dilemma genuinely moving. In fact, he comes close to sentimentality, just the reverse of his detached and satirical tone earlier in the story.

The little body lay upon one side, with one soiled cheek upon one soiled hand, the other hand tucked away among the rags to make it warm, the other cheek washed clean and white at last, as for a kiss from one of God's great angels. It was observed—though nothing was thought of it at the time, the body being as yet unidentified—that the little fellow was lying upon the grave of Hetty Parlow. The grave, however, had not opened to receive him. That is a circumstance which, without actual irreverence, one may wish had been ordered otherwise.

Bierce does finally get "A Baby Tramp" under control, but the effort is costly. There is no doubt that he responded to the image of the homeless orphan, but he shows a great reluctance to give in to his real feelings. In his desire to avoid committing himself, he resorts to an irreverent, off-hand humor that only shows how ill at ease he was with his subject. This same uncertainty occurs in his attitude toward the supernatural. After telling us that the revelers all knew Hetty Parlow and that "they had merry-made on coffee and lemonade only," he feels constrained to add, "of course one does not have to believe all that." He was equally unsure of his protagonist.

Unity and singleness of impression, which Bierce

prized in the short story, are the very qualities that gave him trouble in his nonmilitary fiction. In the war stories he was usually able to achieve both. The war itself provided a microcosm ideally suited to his obsessive theme, a tight symbolic pattern that defined his despairing insights and gave them a coherent dramatic form. Although the pattern is as inflexible (and finally as monotonous) as the conceptions it embodies, it does give these stories their characteristic economy of detail and metaphorical precision. There are seldom any false starts or loose ends in Bierce's war fiction. Everything fits, everything is compressed, controlled by a single point of view. Furthermore, Bierce's attitude toward his protagonists is consistently sympathetic, partly because of a nostalgic fondness for soldiers, but mainly because their ordeal projects his own frustration and disillusionment. It is their origin in deeply personal, inward experience that gives the war tales their authority and their often rich overtones of meaning. In the nonmilitary stories, on the other hand, Bierce is most apt to stumble as a writer. The idiosyncratic realm of blasted hopes and dreams is replaced by a "conventional" world of terror and the supernatural in which Bierce is more often guided by the traditions of the genre than by his own insights and feelings.

Chapter V

OWL CREEK BRIDGE: "A LESSON IN PERSPECTIVE"

BIERCE'S MOST FAMOUS STORY—the best one he ever wrote—is "An Occurrence at Owl Creek Bridge."[1] In its controlling conception and design it resembles most of his war stories; there is the same ironic disparity between reason and imagination, thought and feeling, the same journey through a haunted forest, the dream of happiness and fulfilled desire, followed by the shattering realization that the only possible human condition is one of defeat and death. And once again it is this empirical knowledge which destroys the products of the creative imagination. Literally and symbolically the trap springs shut on Peyton Farquhar, as he swings "gently from side to side beneath the timbers of the Owl Creek bridge," his neck broken, his lovely illusion of escape and reunion with his wife a mocking dream. Yet somehow, these familiar elements, so recurrent in Bierce's war fiction, are brought to a kind of final perfection, as if Bierce had found the ideal formula for embodying his despairing insights. "An Occurrence at Owl Creek Bridge" is an outstanding story for several reasons, but chiefly because Bierce entered so fully into the imaginative life of his protagonist. As a result, the story becomes as vivid and convincing, and as charged with compressed symbolic energy, as Farquhar's hallucination. Paradoxically, the deceptive illusion, which occurs in a matter of seconds, *seems* more real than the actual execution, with its statuelike soldiers and officers and the silent intensity of their preparations. For once, at least, Bierce was able to put salt "upon the tail of a dream's elusive spirit."

At the beginning of the story Bierce makes it clear that Farquhar is about as "trapped" as any man can be. Standing in the middle of the bridge with hands tied behind him, a rope about his neck "attached to a stout cross–timber above his head," the condemned spy is surrounded by seven soldiers, two of whom guard either end of the railroad bridge. A short distance away on the river bank stands "a single company of infantry in line." Everything is conducted in eerie silence; the soldiers stare "stonily, motionless," the sentinels "might have been statues to adorn the bridge"; the captain in charge stands "with folded arms, silent." Even the order that drops Farquhar through the railroad ties to his death is given by a slight nod of the head. As he tries "to fix his last thoughts upon his wife and children," Farquhar is conscious of only one sound, a "metallic percussion like the stroke of a blacksmith's hammer upon the anvil." The noise becomes unbearably loud, yet "as slow as the tolling of a death knell" –and that is exactly what it is, for "what he heard was the ticking of his watch." Time runs out on Peyton Farquhar, although in the strange quiet of the scene and the concentrated intensity of his thoughts it appears to cease altogether. The empirical fact is the ticking watch, the destructive life in time; opposed to it is the beautiful dream of escape and freedom, the subjective reality that would conquer time and all human limitations.

"If I could free my hands," he thought, "I might throw off the noose and spring into the stream. By diving I could evade the bullets and, swimming vigorously, reach the bank, take the woods and get away home."

Like the fatal ticking of the watch, the stream below is "racing madly," but to Farquhar, "how slowly it appeared to move!" The spy, of course, never reaches its "swirling water." He, not time, hangs suspended over Owl Creek, and in the final image of his body swinging "gently from side to side," like the pendulum on a clock, Bierce finds the ideal symbol of man betrayed by the "pitiless perfection of the divine, eternal plan," trapped by a world that seems to promise so much yet give so little. What Farquhar plunges into is the depths of his own subconscious. His thoughts of escape are not rational plans; they originate in the instinct for self-preservation, but represent as well all instinctive desire, all imaginary dreams that allow man to control his destiny and achieve his goals. As Bierce tells us: "these thoughts . . . were flashed into the doomed man's brain rather than evolved from it," and their compelling power and vitality become the substance of the story. Like that promising song of the mockingbird, however, they are "to sense" only, as reason always reveals.

Instead of juxtaposing the dream and the reality throughout, as he does in many stories, Bierce makes us submit to the power of the irrational imagination by turning Farquhar's innermost thoughts and feelings into a seemingly real tale of daring escape. Moreover, it is the kind of tale we would *like* to believe because Farquhar himself is such an attractive figure: brave, sensitive, highly intelligent.

His features were good—a straight nose, firm mouth, broad forehead, from which his long, dark hair was combed straight back, falling behind his ears to the collar of his well-fitting frock-coat. He wore a mustache and pointed beard, but no whiskers; his eyes were large and dark gray, and had a kindly expression which one would hardly have expected in one whose neck was in the hemp. Evidently this was no vulgar assassin.

It is the tragic waste of such a man which engages our sympathies. A wealthy Southerner, Farquhar is made still more sympathetic by the fact that he was deliberately deceived into trying to destroy the Owl Creek Bridge, for which he is executed by the Union soldiers. Before the action of the story, a Federal scout, disguised as a Confederate, had ridden up to Farquhar's plantation and told him of the bridge's importance to the Union cause. Before he rode off as mysteriously as he came, he even hinted that the driftwood caught against its pilings "would burn like tow." Thus Farquhar is doomed from the beginning, the idea of helping the South planted in his mind by an enemy who, presumably, intends to confiscate Farquhar's property once he has been hanged as a spy. His act, in turn, was motivated by a "longing for the release of his energies, the larger life of the soldier, the opportunity for distinction."

Once we plunge with Farquhar into the timeless realm of the subconscious, the story becomes simultaneously as real, and as unreal, as all our dreams. Bierce handles this ambiguity with flawless tact and balances the entire story on the polarities of our response. Reading quickly or casually, one is easily convinced that Farquhar has, in fact, escaped, and the ending comes as a stunning shock. Reading deliberately—that is, with the mind alert for the rational "facts" of the situation—one realizes that it is only a vivid dream. Somehow the reader is made to participate in the split between imagination and reason, to *feel* that the escape is real while he *knows* that it is not. What we want from the story and what we get from it are two different things; like Farquhar, we hang suspended between two worlds. What makes the whole affair so apparently real are the "sensations" of the spy—the "sense of suffocation," "of congestion," the desperate need of air, the "roaring" of the water in his ears as he struggles to free his hands and dislodge the rope. All this, however, is imagined in the few seconds consumed by his drop: "The intellectual part of his nature was already effaced; he had power only to feel, and feeling was torment." Farquhar is the typical Bierce hero, victim of acute sensations and the tricks they play on him. Some of the sensations suggest the actual circumstances while simultaneously reinforcing the illusion. For example, Farquhar, imagining himself weightless in the water, feels that he is swinging "through unthinkable arcs of oscillation, like a vast pendulum," that he is "without material substance," that "all was cold and dark."

All of the spy's "physical senses" are "preternaturally keen and alert" and give his experiences a deceptive concreteness which, upon close inspection, is seen to be impossible. Breaking the surface of the water, his eyes "blinded by the sunlight," Farquhar can see the trees of the forest, "the leaves and the veining of each leaf," the "prismatic colors in all the dewdrops upon a million blades of grass." Even the "strokes of the water-spiders' legs" make "audible music" "like oars which had lifted their boat." Yet this very concreteness gives the escape an authentic ring of truth. Excited soldiers, silhouetted "against the blue sky," shout and gesticulate, Farquhar is spun and buffeted by the current, shots splatter all around him and he dives "as deeply as he could." As he rises for air he meets "shining bits of metal, singularly flattened, oscillating slowly downward." When one drops down his collar "it was uncomfortably warm and he snatched it out." It is this kind of specific detail that keeps persuading the reader that perhaps the impossible has happened, that the rope did break and that soon Farquhar will be safe in the forest. Whirled downstream, Farquhar finds himself momentarily hidden "behind a projecting point which concealed him from his enemies." He blesses the sand in gratitude for his escape. The world is transfigured, a new Eden in which the trees "were giant garden plants," the forest suffused in "a strange roseate light," filled with "the music of aeolian harps." Only the "whiz and rattle of grapeshot" makes him leave this "enchanting spot." Springing to his feet, Farquhar "plunged into the forest."

What was an Eden by day becomes at night something weirdly ambiguous, a nightmare of flight rather than a dream of safety. As in "A Tough Tussle," the forest symbolizes the haunted mind of its occupant, victimized by the irrational imagination and the contents it throws up from the depths of the subconscious. Its possibilities are endless: "The forest seemed interminable; nowhere did he discover a break in it . . . He had not known that he lived in so wild a region. There was something uncanny in the revelation." With a dream's irrational logic, a road suddenly materializes. It is "untraveled," yet runs "wide and straight as a city street" through the forest. The frightening thing about this seeming avenue of escape is that it leads nowhere–it terminates "on the horizon in a point, like a diagram in a lesson in perspective." Above his head Farquhar sees "strange constellations" and is certain they are "arranged in some order which had a secret and malign significance." Instead of being assured of his safety, he appears to doubt the validity of his own dream, as if he were now on the threshold of consciousness. He is haunted by ambiguous sensations, poised between the terror of impending death and the seductive dream of reunion with his family.

"An Occurrence at Owl Creek Bridge" is itself a "lesson in perspective," simultaneously scaled to the life in time and the life where time does not exist, to the appearance of things and to the reality of things. As he walks down the eerie road, the fugitive from destructive realities is conscious that his neck is "horribly swollen." To relieve his parched tongue, he thrusts it into the cool night air. The drop has taken place; Farquhar is at the end of his rope. Yet he is still in the haunted forest of acute sensation: "how softly the turf had carpeted the untraveled avenue–he could no longer feel the roadway beneath his feet!" In the split second before his neck is broken, "he stands at the gate of his own home." To convey the intensity of this last sensation–of desire fulfilled–Bierce shifts to the historical present as he describes Farquhar's wife, "fresh and cool and sweet," descending the veranda steps. "At the bottom of the steps she stands waiting, with a smile of ineffable joy, an attitude of matchless grace and dignity." But she is only the beautiful dream of happiness that always eludes us. This was the lesson Haïta the shepherd learned. Farquhar learns it now, for as he "springs forward with extended arms" the vision disappears, obliterated by the cracking neck bone, the "darkness and silence."

This is the way it must always end in Bierce's fiction. The dreamer is "awakened" to a real world of futility and death, just as Bierce, who dreamed of romantic exciting experience in his haunted forest, awoke to the reductive realities of the Gilded Age and his limitations as an artist. Like Peyton Farquhar, Bierce longed "for the release of his energies, the larger life of the soldier, the opportunity for distinction." He became, like Farquhar, "a civilian who was at heart a soldier." In a poem called "My Day of Life," [2] Bierce reviews the rich experience that comes to him in dreams at daybreak:

> And, O I've dreamed so many things!
>   One hardly can unravel
> The tangled web of visionings
> That slumber-of-the-morning brings:
>   Play, study, work and travel;

The love of women (mostly those
Were fairest that were newest);
Hard knocks from friends and other foes:
Compacts with men (my memory shows
The deadest are the truest);

War—what a hero I became
By merely dreaming battle!
Athwart the field of letters, Fame
Blared through the brass my weary name
With an ominous death-rattle.

Such an eternity of thought
Within a minute's fraction!
Such phantoms out of nothing wrought,
And fading suddenly to naught
As I awake to action!

They scamper each into its hole,
These dreams of my begetting.
They've had their moment; take, my soul,
Thy day of life. . . . Gods! this is droll—
That thieving sun is setting! [3]

If the next-to-last stanza is the unwritten epigraph of "An Occurrence at Owl Creek Bridge," the poem itself describes the pattern of Bierce's fiction as a whole, for it fuses the knowledge and the dream into a bitter awareness of "phantoms out of nothing wrought."

"We are all," Bierce remarked, "dominated by our imaginations and our views are creatures of our viewpoints." [4] Bierce's own views were always precariously balanced between the polarities of his response to art and to life. One viewpoint saw imagination as man's greatest endowment; another saw it as the curse of illusions painfully exposed. The romantic called for the romance "that owes no allegiance to the God of

Things as They Are"; the cynical realist prided himself on being "devoid of all delusions." Such a dual conception determines the form of almost every story Bierce wrote and the obsessive nature of his irony. Only in the war tales could he give his divided sensibility a coherent form and meaning, but that is all he could do. "An Occurrence at Owl Creek Bridge" turns his dilemma into a work of art by making the deceptive imagination more "real" than its final defeat; a few other stories approach its excellence. Bierce, however, can only tell us the same thing over and over so that there is no range or richness of conception in his art. His fiction is further limited since he never applied his insights to American experience as a whole nor to issues larger than his own crisis. In his poorest stories his inability to integrate his attitudes shows up as a loss of control over his tone. The opposing points of view are directed *at* the story, instead of inhering in it. Irony moves toward satire, tragedy or pathos threatens to become farce. Bierce either ceases to take his imaginative creations or his protagonists seriously, or else reacts flippantly to death and suffering. His bitterness causes him to deny his own creative impulses, as if the out-and-out satirist were trying his hand at serious fiction. Another symptom of his artistic collapse is the number of conventional ghost stories Bierce wrote, in which he appears to be seeking merely diversion or escape instead of a significant engagement with experience. Eventually he rejected fiction altogether as the sense of futility and the failure to reach an audience grew. As he once wrote, referring to the relation between thought and style: "A mind without utterance is like a lake without an outlet: though fed with mountain springs and unfailing rivers, its waters do not long keep sweet." [5]

Notes

INTRODUCTION

1. Walter Neale, *Life of Ambrose Bierce*, pp. 380–81.
2. Unfortunately, the author has been unable to locate Bennett's article which appeared in *The New Age* under the pseudonym "Jacob Tonson." It is quoted extensively, however, in "The Underground Reputation of Ambrose Bierce," *Current Literature*, XLVII (September 1909), 279–81.
3. Carey McWilliams, *Ambrose Bierce: A Biography*, p. 3.
4. "Ambrose Bierce on the Owl Creek Bridge," *New Yorker*, December 8, 1951, pp. 144, 147.
5. *The Letters of Ambrose Bierce*, ed. Bertha Clark Pope, p. 148. Cited hereafter as *Letters*.
6. R. Barry, *The Mentor*, IX (June 1921), 34. See also Francis Gribble, "The Ambrose Bierce Mystery," *The Biblio*, IV (July 1924), 673–75; Carey McWilliams, "The Mystery of Ambrose Bierce," *The American Mercury*, XXII (March 1931), 330–37; H. L. Mencken, "The Ambrose Bierce Mystery," *The American Mercury*, XVIII (September 1929), 124–26.
7. C. Hartley Grattan, *The Reviewer*, V (October 1925), 103–08.
8. New York, 1924, p. 275.
9. *Their Day in Court*, p. 256. George Jean Nathan has remarked of Pollard as a critic: "In his day, Percy discovered geniuses by the wholesale and by the freight carload. The only trouble with the great majority of his geniuses was that they didn't seem to have much noticeable talent. But that never deterred Percy, as a glance through his critical manifestoes will attest." *The World of G. J. Nathan*, ed. Charles Angoff, p. 84.
10. William M. Clemens, "The Art of Ambrose Bierce," *The Biblio*, IV (July 1924), 676.
11. Barry, *The Mentor*, 34.
12. "The Satirist in Vacuo," *The Freeman*, I (August 1920), 516.

13. "Bierce in His Brilliant Obscurity," *New York Times*, October 11, 1936, p. 2.

14. "Ambrose, Son of Marcus Aurelius," *Atlantic Monthly*, XVII (September 1929), 36.

15. *New York Times*, October 11, 1936, p. 2.

16. *Current Literature*, XLVII (September 1909), 281.

17. Alfred Kazin, *On Native Grounds: An Interpretation of Modern American Prose Literature*, p. 194.

18. Frank Monaghan, "Ambrose Bierce and the Authorship of *The Monk and the Hangman's Daughter*," *American Literature*, II (January 1931), 338.

19. This edition, published by G. P. Putnam's Sons, was the first American edition to use the title *In the Midst of Life*, under which it has appeared in all subsequent editions. The first English edition of Bierce's stories, however, published by Chatto and Windus (London, 1892), used the title *In the Midst of Life*. See Vincent Starrett, *Ambrose Bierce, a Bibliography*, p. 40.

20. *The Collected Works of Ambrose Bierce*. Cited hereafter as *Works*. Only about 1,250 sets were initially printed, the cheapest of which sold for $30. For details about the publication of the *Works*, and of Bierce's relations with publishers generally, see Neale, *Life of Ambrose Bierce*, pp. 409–28.

21. McWilliams, *Ambrose Bierce*, p. vii.

22. See chap. xiii, "Bierce and the Charnel House," pp. 222–35.

23. McWilliams, *Ambrose Bierce*, pp. 235, 12.

24. For an illuminating article on this controversy, see n. 18 above. Monaghan, who compared the German original with Bierce's version, finds that Bierce contributed little to the work except for an ironic ending and minor stylistic changes.

25. *New Yorker*, December 8, 1951, p. 144.

26. Josephine Clifford McCrackin, *The Woman Who Lost Him and Tales of the Army Frontier*, p. 34.

27. "The Shadow Maker," *The American Mercury*, VI (September 1925), 10.

28. E. Boyd, Review of *Bitter Bierce* by C. Hartley Grattan, *Outlook*, CLI (March 1929), 470.

29. Bierce, *Wasp*, December 12, 1885. Quoted in Fatout, *Ambrose Bierce*, p. 146.

30. "Ashes of the Beacon: An Historical Mongraph Written in 4930," *Works*, I, 31.

31. *The Golden Day: A Study in American Literature and Culture*, p 89.

32. "The Moonlit Road," *The Collected Writings of Ambrose Bierce*, introd. Clifton Fadiman, p. 419. All quotations from Bierce's fiction and *The Devil's Dictionary* are taken from this edition, cited hereafter as *Collected Writings*. It is presently the most widely available. The twelve-volume *Works* is the definitive edition but too scarce to be used as the source for Bierce's fiction. The Fadiman volume is an unaltered reprint (paperback) of the 1946 edition published by Citadel Press.

33. See Allan Kelly's contemporary sketch of the *Examiner* in Ella Sterling Cummins, *The Story of the Files: A Review of California Writers and Literature*, pp. 421–25. According to Kelly, "Bierce . . . printed originally in the *Examiner* most of the short stories and verses contained in his later published volumes" (p. 422). See also McWilliams, *Ambrose Bierce*, pp. 126, 210.

34. "Personal Memories of Ambrose Bierce," *Bookman*, XL (February 1915), 656–57.

35. Grant C. Knight, *The Critical Period in American Literature*, p. 89.

36. *The Devil's Dictionary, Collected Writings*, p. 338.

37. "The Realm of the Unreal," *Collected Writings*, p. 511.

38. See chaps. i ("The Titaness") and vi ("The American Magazines"), *The Mauve Decade* in *Hanna, Crane, and The Mauve Decade*.

39. Ibid., p. 39.

40. "The Short Story," *Works*, X, 241.

41. *The Novel: What It Is*, p. 30.

42. *The Devil's Dictionary, Collected Writings*, p. 338.

43. Ruth Guthrie Harding, "Mr. Boythorn-Bierce," *Bookman*, LXI (August 1925), 638. Despite the heavy sentiment in this article, Miss Guthrie is essentially correct in remarking of Bierce: "his genuine bitterness was that of a bruised idealist. Holding the fragments of dreams is a much more terrible business than hating what broke the dreams. I think

Bierce never ceased yearning over his, and he put them away in his heart instead of forgetting them" (p. 643).

44. *The Freeman,* I (August 1920), 516.

45. Upton Sinclair, "My Friend, George Sterling," *Overland Monthly*, LXXXV (November 1927), 365.

CHAPTER I

1. "To Train a Writer," *Works,* X, 77.

2. *The Devil's Dictionary, Collected Writings,* pp. 205, 292.

3. "Epigrams," *Works,* VIII, 375.

4. *Collected Writings,* pp. 207–08.

5. San Francisco *Examiner,* August 31, 1889, quoted in McWilliams, *Ambrose Bierce,* p. 42.

6. "A Son of the Gods," *Collected Writings,* p. 29.

7. "Religion," *Works,* XI, 244.

8. "The Ancestral Bond," *Works,* XI, 332. See also "The Death Penalty," *Works,* XI, 210–24, and "Crime and Its Correctives," *Works,* XI, 187–98.

9. "The Ancestral Bond," *Works,* XI, 332.

10. "For Standing Room," *Works,* IX, 370, 371.

11. *Works,* XI, 145–49.

12. *The Devil's Dictionary, Collected Writings,* p. 221.

13. Herman Scheffauer said of Bierce's fiction: "In his tales it afforded him pleasure to conjure up a merciless and devilish destiny for his puppets that entangled them in frightful dilemmas, and then to contemplate their writhings through the perspective of an art that had become objective to the point of inhumanity." Quoted in Neale, *Life of Ambrose Bierce,* p. 230.

14. *Works,* XI, 147.

15. Ibid., pp. 148–49.

16. *Collected Writings,* pp. 30–40.

17. *Works,* XI, 329.

18. In *The Devil's Dictionary* (*Collected Writings,* p. 192), Bierce defines an "accident" as "an inevitable occurrence due to the action of immutable natural laws."

19. See Robert Littell, "Bitter Bierce," *Read America First,* pp. 183–88. Littell says of Bierce's fiction: "It is the kind of

story which, from the very beginning, is built up and hammered together for the sake of the final twist, the dramatic denouement which in Bierce's case was often as violent as the kick of a mule in the reader's face" (p. 187). The implication of Littell's statement is misleading, for it suggests that Bierce invariably began with some trick ending in mind and then wrote his story around it. While it is true that Bierce seems to hold some final horror or irony in reserve until the last moment, what Bierce really starts with is a set of premises from which only a certain kind of conclusion can follow.

20. *Collected Writings*, pp. 99–104.

21. Leroy J. Nations, "Ambrose Bierce: the Gray Wolf of American Letters," *South Atlantic Quarterly*, XXV (July 1926), 258.

22. See "Taking Oneself Off," *Works*, XI, 338–44. Bierce felt that "suicide is always courageous. We call it courage in a soldier merely to face death—say to lead a forlorn hope—although he has a chance of life. . . . But the suicide does more than face death; he incurs it, and with a certainty, not of glory, but of reproach. If that is not courage we must reform our vocabulary" (p. 341). Walter Neale claimed that Bierce never went into Mexico at all, but took his own life in the vicinity of the Grand Canyon. For a discussion of this theory see his *Life of Ambrose Bierce*, pp. 429–49.

23. "Taking Oneself Off," pp. 338, 343.

24. See Bierce's letter to Josephine McCrackin, September 13, 1913, *Letters*, pp. 195–96. Telling her that he was about to "go into Mexico with a pretty definite purpose, which, however, is not at present disclosable," he added: "You must try to forgive my obstinacy in not 'perishing' where I am. I want to be where something worthwhile is going on, or where nothing whatever is going on. Most of what is going on in your own country is exceedingly distasteful to me." He hoped that she might live as long as she wished and "then pass smilingly into the darkness—the good, good darkness."

25. *Collected Writings*, pp. 74–80.

26. Ibid., pp. 59–64.

27. Ibid., pp. 89–94, 95–99.

28. In *The Devil's Dictionary* (*Collected Writings*, p. 232), Bierce defines "enthusiasm" as "a distemper of youth,

curable by small doses of repentance in connection with outward applications of experience."

29. *The Devil's Dictionary*, *Collected Writings*, p. 194.

30. "Epigrams," *Works*, VIII, 375.

31. *The Devil's Dictionary*, *Collected Writings*, pp. 322–23. The distinction Bierce makes here between the "past" and the "future" is an underlying motif in his fiction. The past he saw as "a region of sobs . . . dark with sorrow and disappointment"; the future was always "bright with prosperity and joy." Dividing them was "a moving line called the Present," and as it moved, the past was "continually effacing" the future. Many of Bierce's war stories are constructed on this linear principle; that is, the protagonist takes a one-way trip to the end of bright hopes and forward-looking dreams.

Although the contrast between a former time of dreams and joy and a present despair is typical of romantic literature in general, the writer Bierce most immediately suggests is Poe. In Poe's poetry we find a similar preoccupation with the theme of displacement, a similar sense of disparity between lovely dreams and reductive realities. The imagination could take the mind away from the prosaic present and into the realm of dreams, but never for long. As Poe says in "The Happiest Day, The Happiest Hour":

> The happiest day—the happiest hour
> My seared and blighted heart hath known,
> The highest hope of pride and power,
> I feel hath flown.

The movement away from the present, followed by a return to its limiting conditions, occurs also in such poems as "A Dream Within a Dream" and "Romance." Both Poe and Bierce, in treating the world of here and now, find, "That the play is the tragedy, 'Man,'/And its hero the Conqueror Worm." Because it is a world that kills the imagination and deadens the spirit, it is characteristically defined in terms of death and horror. The similarity between Bierce and Poe results from a striking similarity of temperament, and not, as several critics have claimed, from any conscious attempt by Bierce to "imitate" Poe or his effects.

32. *The Devil's Dictionary*, *Collected Writings*, p. 236.

33. "Chickamauga," *Collected Writings*, pp. 18–23.

34. Review of *In the Midst of Life*, *The Nation*, LXVI (March 1898), 225.

35. *Collected Writings*, p. 331.

36. Ibid., p. 203.

37. *Works*, XI, 328–29.

38. In a letter to a young girl, dated June 20, 1902, Bierce advised: "You must not expect too much happiness, and you *must* be prepared for disappointment and disillusion. That will be hard for you to understand now; it will (unfortunately) be clearer to you later." "A Collection of Bierce Letters," *University of California Chronicle*, XXXIV (January 1932), 40. Virtually all of Bierce's war stories end, as does "Chickamauga," with some "revelation" of "disappointment and disillusion."

39. "On the Uses of Euthanasia," *Works*, IX, 327.

40. "New Letters of Ambrose Bierce," *Opinion*, II (May 1930), 4.

41. Neale, *Life of Ambrose Bierce*, p. 157.

42. *The Philosophy of Despair*, pp. 18–19.

43. *Collected Writings*, pp. 54–58.

44. See, for example, H. L. Mencken, "Ambrose Bierce," *Prejudices: Sixth Series*, pp. 259–65. Mencken's own temperament led him to see Bierce exclusively in terms of sardonic wit and caused him to misjudge the serious fiction. Thus he claims, incorrectly, that Bierce emerged from the war with a "cynical delight" in its horror, and that "death to him was not something repulsive but a sort of low comedy—the last act of a squalid and rib-rocking buffoonery" (p. 262).

45. "On the Uses of Euthanasia," *Works*, IX, 335–36.

46. "Prayer," *Works*, IV, 375.

47. "Immortality," *Works*, XI, 249.

48. "Religion," *Works*, XI, 228–29.

49. Otto Friedrich, "The Passion of Death in Ambrose Bierce," *Zero*, II (Spring 1956), 79.

CHAPTER II

1. On Bierce's experiences in the war and their effect on him, see McWilliams, *Ambrose Bierce*, pp. 28–64. See also Neale, *Life of Ambrose Bierce*, pp. 69–86.

2. Fatout, *Ambrose Bierce*, pp. 314–15.

3. In 1866, having applied for a commission in the regular army, Bierce joined his former commander, General W. B. Hazen, on an inspection tour of western military posts. For an account of this trip see Bierce's essay "Across the Plains," *Works*, I, 360–69. When the party reached San Francisco, Bierce received a reply to his application: "finding myself appointed to a second lieutenancy in the Regular Army, ingratitude, more strong than traitors' arms, quite vanquished me: I resigned, parted from Hazen more in sorrow than in anger and remained in California" (p. 364).

4. *New Yorker*, December 8, 1951, p. 150.

5. *Works*, XI, 93, 95.

6. "The Hesitating Veteran," *Works*, IV, 118.

7. "A Bivouac of the Dead," *Works*, XI, 398.

8. *The Devil's Dictionary*, *Collected Writings*, pp. 390–91.

9. *Ambrose Bierce*, p. 141.

10. *Works*, I, 269.

11. McWilliams, *Ambrose Bierce*, p. 38.

12. *Works*, I, 234, 236–37, 257.

13. Ibid., p. 225.

14. Ibid., p. 232.

15. After one such visit Bierce wrote to George Sterling: "My trip . . . has done my health good—and my heart too. It was a 'sentimental journey' in a different sense from Sterne's. Do you know, George, the charm of a new emotion? Of course you do, but at my age I had thought it impossible. Well, I had it repeatedly. Bedad, I think of going again into my old 'theatre of war,' and setting up a cabin there and living the few days that remain to me in meditation and sentimentalizing." *Letters*, p. 76.

16. *Letters*, p. 204.

17. *The Devil's Dictionary*, *Collected Writings*, p. 295.

18. "Epigrams," *Works*, VIII, 347.

19. *Works*, I, 255.

20. Ibid.

21. Ibid.

22. Ibid., p. 261.

23. Ibid., p. 262.

24. Ibid. Bierce's daughter once wrote of her father: "Soldiering in the Civil War, he had seen many shattered bodies

and could never rid himself of the horror of them." Helen Bierce, "Ambrose Bierce at Home," *The American Mercury*, XXX (December 1933), 458.

25. *Works*, I, 232–33.

26. Ibid., p. 233.

27. Howard P. Lovecraft, *Supernatural Horror in Literature*, p. 53.

28. *The Devil's Dictionary*, *Collected Writings*, p. 323.

29. One of Bierce's supernatural stories also deals with identical twins and the theme of ambiguous identity; see "One of Twins," *Collected Writings*, pp. 445–50. The narrator tells us that no one "could distinguish between him and me if we chose to seem alike. . . . I speak of my brother John, but I am not at all sure that his name was not Henry and mine John. We were regularly christened, but afterward, in the very act of tattooing us . . . the operator lost his reckoning; and although I bear upon my forearm a small 'H' and he bore a 'J,' it is by no means certain that the letters ought not to have been transposed" (p. 445).

30. *Works*, X, 127–31.

31. Neale, *Life of Ambrose Bierce*, p. 158.

32. Quoted in McWilliams, *Ambrose Bierce*, pp. 67–68.

33. Bierce to Blanche Partington, January 14, 1893, *Letters*, p 24.

34. *Works*, X, 76, 77.

35. *The Devil's Dictionary*, *Collected Writings*, p. 337.

36. Bierce defines "moral" as "conforming to a local and mutable standard of right. Having the quality of general expediency." Ibid., p. 309. See "The Value of Truth," *Works*, IX, 179–84. Here Bierce claims that "morality has, and can have, no other basis than expediency" (p. 180).

37. "Epigrams," *Works*, VIII, 375.

38. *Letters*, p. 201.

39. *The Freeman*, I, 514.

40. Bailey Millard, *Bookman*, XL, 657.

41. *Collected Writings*, pp. 24–29.

42. *Ambrose Bierce* p. 45.

43. *The Wasp*, July 14, 1883. Quoted in McWilliams, *Ambrose Bierce*, p. 45.

CHAPTER III

1. *Works,* X, 254. Most of Bierce's literary criticism appears in this volume.

2. Ibid., p. 253.

3. "On Reading New Books," *Works,* X, 67.

4. See, for example, "Poetry and Verse," *Works,* X, 267–69; see also "On Literary Criticism," *Works,* X, 27–28 *et passim.*

5. "The Short Story," *Works,* X, 245.

6. Ibid., p. 244.

7. "Youth looks forward, for nothing is behind; Age backward, for nothing is before." "Epigrams," *Works,* VIII, 368.

8. "Visions of the Night," *Works,* X, 122, 123.

9. Ibid.

10. Ibid., p. 125.

11. Preface to *The House of the Seven Gables, The Complete Novels and Selected Tales of Nathaniel Hawthorne,* ed. Norman Holmes Pearson, p. 243.

12. *Collected Writings,* p. 338.

13. Norris' essay bearing this title is found in his book *The Responsibilities of the Novelist and Other Literary Essays,* pp. 213–20.

14. Ibid.

15. Ibid., p. 214.

16. Ibid., p. 220. There is, of course, a fundamental difference between Norris' views on the romance and those of Bierce. Whereas Norris—and certainly Hawthorne—saw the romance as a way of coming to grips with the deeper and more permanent aspects of man's experience (with "the problems of life"), Bierce regarded it as an amoral, autonomous form which served no didactic, or even social, function. To Bierce, the freedom of the romance was a freedom *from* the material world and the conditions of man's existence; to Norris, the romance provided a freedom for their fullest expression and investigation.

17. "The Novel," *Works,* X, 22.

18. *The Devil's Dictionary, Collected Writings,* p. 350. Like many writers—Poe, for example—Bierce made a number

of critical judgments which were really thinly disguised defenses of his own practices and limitations as an artist. Bierce's friend Gertrude Atherton once told him that he disliked the novel mainly because he was incapable of writing one. See Atherton, *Adventures of a Novelist*, p. 204.

19. "The Novel," *Works*, X, 19.
20. *The Devil's Dictionary*, *Collected Writings*, pp. 313–14.
21. Ibid., p. 314.
22. "The Novel," *Works*, X, 19.
23. "The Short Story," *Works*, X, 239.
24. See W. D. Howells, *Criticism and Fiction*, pp. 128, 187. Judging from his frequent jibes, Bierce was quite familiar with Howells' literary criticism, whose whole aesthetic could not have been more opposed to his own. For example, one would almost think Howells had Bierce in mind when he wrote: "The art which . . . disdains the office of teacher is one of the last refuges of the aristocratic spirit which is disappearing from politics and society, and is now seeking to shelter itself in aesthetics. The pride of caste is becoming the pride of taste; but as before, it is averse to the mass of men; it consents to know them only in some conventionalized and artificial guise. It seeks to withdraw itself, to stand aloof; to be distinguished, and not to be identified. Democracy in literature is the reverse of all this" (*Criticism and Fiction*, p. 187). If Bierce was anything, he was an "aristocratic spirit" who wished "to stand aloof," who was decidedly "averse to the mass of men." The last thing he wanted was "to be identified" with his age or its prevailing tastes.
25. *The Devil's Dictionary*, *Collected Writings*, p. 350.
26. Ibid.
27. "The Short Story," *Works*, X, 237.
28. "The Novel," *Works*, X, 23.
29. "The Short Story," *Works*, X, 247.
30. Ibid., p. 248.
31. Ibid.
32. "The Novel," *Works*, X, 22, 23.
33. Quoted in Neale, *Life of Ambrose Bierce*, p. 372.
34. "Fin de Siècle," *Works*, IX, 141.
35. *Works*, X, 269.
36. Ibid.

37. Ibid., p. 270. Cf. Poe's "Sonnet–to Science" which makes the same point.

> Science! true daughter of Old Time thou art!
> Who alterest all things with thy peering eyes.
> Why preyest thou thus upon the poet's heart,
> Vulture, whose wings are dull realities?
> How should he love thee? or how deem thee wise,
> Who wouldst not leave him in his wandering
> To seek for treasure in the jewelled skies,
> Albeit he soared with an undaunted wing?
> Hast thou not dragged Diana from her car?
> And driven the Hamadryad from the wood
> To seek a shelter in some happier star?
> Hast thou not torn the Naiad from her flood,
> The Elfin from the green grass, and from me
> The summer dream beneath the tamarind tree?

38. *The Devil's Dictionary, Collected Writings*, p. 218, 267.

39. Ibid., p. 288. Neale comments: "He always took himself seriously. No mirth; unless a 'smile' of a kind peculiar to himself–sardonic, macabre, which would cause the onlooker to shiver slightly–might indicate a type of mirth" (*Life of Ambrose Bierce*, p. 209).

40. *The Story of the Files*, p. 422.

41. Matthew Josephson, *Portrait of the Artist as American*, p. 160.

42. Wilson Follett, "America's Neglected Satirist," *The Dial*, LXV (July 1918), 52.

43. Letter to Blanche Partington, August 15, 1892, *Letters*, p. 7.

44. "A Collection of Bierce Letters," *Univeristy of California Chronicle*, XXXIV (January 1932), 47.

45. Letter to Herman Scheffauer, July 1903, *Letters*, p. 68.

46. "Who Are Great," *Works*, X, 249–50.

47. *In Our Second Century, from an Editor's Notebook*, p. 153. See also pp. 152–78.

48. October 21, 1903, *Letters*, pp. 78–79.

49. March 15, 1902, *Letters*, p. 53.

50. June 16, 1905, *Letters*, p. 111.

51. October 21, 1903, *Letters*, p. 78.

52. "A Thumb-Nail Sketch," *Works*, XII, 307. Bierce was referring to his work for Hearst. Of their curious relationship he remarked: "If ever two men were born to be enemies he and I are they. Each stands for everything that is most disagreeable to the other, yet we never clashed" (p. 306).

53. Letter to Charles Warren Stoddard, February 2, 1874. Unpublished letters.

54. January 8, 1904, *Letters*, p. 83.

55. Quoted in McWilliams, *Ambrose Bierce*, p. 200.

56. *Life of Ambrose Bierce*, pp. 144–45.

57. January 8, 1904, *Letters*, p. 83.

58. October 12, 1903, *Letters*, p. 76.

59. September 21, 1905, "A Collection of Bierce Letters," 41.

60. "The Passing of Satire," *Works*, X, 281–82.

61. Ibid., pp. 283–84.

62. *The Dial*, LXV (July 1918), 51.

63. Letter to Richard Harding Davis, October 12, 1904, *Letters*, p. 102.

64. Review of *In the Midst of Life*, *Atheneum*, February 20, 1892, p. 241.

65. *The Age of Confidence: Life in the Nineties*, p. 14. See also chap. x, "What They Read," pp. 185–209.

66. *Works*, IV, 46–47.

67. See A. J. A. Symons, Introduction to *Ambrose Bierce: Ten Tales*, pp. vii–xiv. Symons was one of the first to recognize Bierce's obsessive concern with his war experience. "Lost in the mass of essays," he writes, "studies in memory may be found, almost stereoscopic in their sharpness, studies in which his mind turned again and again with a fascinated regret to that time when, a brilliant young man, his energies were expressed in action" (p. xii).

68. *Collected Writings*, pp. 469–74. The protagonist, a former lieutenant in General Hazen's brigade, discovers the fatal time lapse when he stumbles on a monument, "brown with age," dedicated to the soldiers "who fell at Stone River, December 31, 1862." McWilliams (*Ambrose Bierce*, pp. 46, 47) notes that Bierce wrote this story long after his other war tales—and after one of his visits to his old battlefields.

CHAPTER IV

1. *Collected Writings*, pp. 793–800.
2. Ibid., pp. 806–10.
3. The stories in "The Parenticide Club" also seem to reflect Bierce's belief that horror was intensified when combined with incongruous humor. In a poem called "Judex Jocosus" (*Works*, IV, 150), he writes:

> We blench when maniacs to dance begin.
> What makes a skull so dreadful is the grin.
> When horrible and ludicrous unite,
> Our sense of humor does but feed our fright.

However interesting as a theory, in practice Bierce's humor undermines the horror instead of enhancing it. Sometimes this occurs unintentionally in some of his ghost stories and spoils the very effect he is ostensibly striving to create.

4. Bierce, introduction to McCrackin, *The Woman Who Lost Him*, p. v.
5. "The Night-Doings at 'Deadman's,'" *Collected Writings*, p. 481.
6. *Dark Conceit: The Making of Allegory*, p. 130.
7. *The Devil's Dictionary*, *Collected Writings*, p. 219.
8. *Collected Writings*, pp. 417–26.
9. See chap. vii, "Polite Literature and Ghosts," and p. 140.
10. *Collected Writings*, pp. 451–60.
11. *The Story of the Files*, p. 212.
12. According to Walter Neale, Bierce "at least half-way believed in ghosts" and attributed his superstition to the influence of his ancestors. (*Life of Ambrose Bierce*, p. 184). In England, Bierce was convinced that he had once encountered the spirit of his friend Tom Hood, who had died a short time before. "I need not attempt to describe my feelings; they were novel and not altogether agreeable. That I had met the spirit of my dead friend; that it had given me recognition, yet not in the old way; that it had then vanished—of these things I had the evidence of my own senses. How strongly this impressed me the beating of my heart attested whenever, for months afterward, that strange meeting came into my

memory." Quoted in McWilliams, *Ambrose Bierce*, pp. 104–05.

13. "Some Disadvantages of Genius," *Works*, X, 296.

14. A. C. Ward, *Aspects of the Modern Short Story*, p. 60. For an article which laboriously traces parallels between Poe's tales and those of Bierce, see Arthur E. Miller, "The Influence of Edgar Allan Poe on Ambrose Bierce," *American Literature*, IV (May 1932), 130–50.

15. *Collected Writings*, p. 248.

16. Ibid., pp. 527–32.

17. "Civilization," *Works*, XI, 52.

18. *Works*, X, 77.

19. *The Devil's Dictionary*, *Collected Writings*, p. 231.

20. Ibid., pp. 438–44.

21. Ibid., pp. 142–48.

22. *California the Wonderful*, p. 350.

23. According to Neale, Bierce was "from his youth until the end of his days . . . beset by a false sense of educational deficiency" and was unreasonably afraid of a man with a college diploma (*Life of Ambrose Bierce*, p. 44). To hide his own lack of formal schooling, Bierce posed as an authority on many subjects with which he had little familiarity, and always tried to avoid situations where he would be "inferior in any regard" (p. 47). The pontifical manner in which he often passed judgment on diverse matters does suggest a man trying to cover up his own uncertainty, as does the endless stream of abusive journalism through which he mounted his attack on the world at large.

24. *Collected Writings*, pp. 475–79.

CHAPTER V

1. *Collected Writings*, pp. 9–18.

2. *Works*, IV, 342–44.

3. Ibid. Significantly, these dreams occur at sunrise—that is, at the dawn of life, the period of youth and forward-looking expectations.

4. "Fin de Siècle," *Works*, IX, 139.

5. "The Matter of Manner," *Works*, X, 60. Because of the compulsive, and ultimately sterile, nature of his own ideas,

Bierce took the curious position that style alone determined literary excellence—that content was unimportant. "In literature, as in all art, manner is everything and matter nothing; I mean that matter, however important, has nothing to do with the *art* of literature; that is a thing apart. In literature it makes very little difference what you say, but a great deal how you say it. It is precisely this thing called style which determines and fixes the place of any written discourse . . ." (p. 63). Such a statement reflects Bierce's wishful thinking and an attempt to rationalize the limitations of his own ideas and attitudes.

Bibliography

BOOKS

Atherton, Gertrude. *Adventures of a Novelist.* New York: Liveright, Inc., 1932.

Beer, Thomas. *Hanna, Crane, and The Mauve Decade.* New York: Alfred A. Knopf, Inc., 1941.

Bierce, Ambrose. *Ambrose Bierce: Ten Tales.* With an introduction by A. J. A. Symons. (First Edition Club.) London, 1925.

———. *Ambrose Bierce's Civil War.* Edited and with an introduction by William McCann. (Gateway Editions.) Chicago: Henry Regnery Co., 1956.

———. *Can Such Things Be?* New York: Cassell Publishing Co., 1893.

———. *The Collected Works of Ambrose Bierce.* 12 vols. New York and Washington: Neale Publishing Co., 1909–12.

———. *The Collected Writings of Ambrose Bierce.* With an introduction by Clifton Fadiman. New York: Citadel Press, 1960.

———. *The Cynic's Word Book.* New York: Doubleday & Company, Inc., 1906.

———. *The Eyes of the Panther.* Edited and with an introduction by Martin Armstrong. (Traveller's Library.) London: Jonathan Cape, 1928.

———. *In the Midst of Life: Tales of Soldiers and Civilians.* With an introduction by George Sterling. (Modern Library edition.) New York: Random House, Inc., 1927.

———. *The Letters of Ambrose Bierce.* Edited by Bertha Clark Pope, with a memoir of George Sterling. San Francisco: The Book Club of California, 1922.

———. *The Shadow on the Dial and other Essays.* Edited by S. O. Howes. San Francisco: A. M. Robertson, 1909.

———. *Tales of Soldiers and Civilians.* San Francisco: E. L. G. Steele, 1891.

———. *Twenty-One Letters of Ambrose Bierce.* Edited by Samuel Loveman. Cleveland: George Kirk, 1922.

———. *Write It Right: A Little Blacklist of Literary Faults.* New York and Washington: Neale Publishing Co., 1909.

Boynton, Percy H. *Literature and American Life*. Boston: Ginn & Company, 1936.

———. "Ambrose Bierce." *More Contemporary Americans*. Chicago: University of Chicago Press, 1927.

Brooks, Van Wyck. *The Confident Years: 1885–1915*. New York: E. P. Dutton Co., Inc., 1952.

———. *Sketches in Criticism*. New York: E. P. Dutton Co., Inc., 1932.

Canby, Henry Seidel. *The Age of Confidence: Life in the Nineties*. New York: Farrar, Straus & Co., Inc., 1934.

———. *Definitions: Essays in Contemporary Criticism*. New York: Harcourt, Brace & World, 1922.

Carter, Everett. *Howells and the Age of Realism*. Philadelphia: J. B. Lippincott Co., 1950.

Chase, Richard. *The American Novel and Its Tradition*. (Doubleday Anchor Books.) Garden City: Doubleday & Company, Inc., 1957.

Commager, Henry Steele. *The American Mind: An Interpretation of American Thought and Character since the 1880's*. New Haven: Yale University Press, 1957.

Cooper, Frederic Taber. "Ambrose Bierce." *Some American Story Tellers*. New York: Holt, Rinehart & Winston, Inc., 1911.

Crawford, F. Marion. *The Novel: What It Is*. New York: The Macmillan Co., 1893.

Cummins, Ella Sterling. *The Story of the Files: A Review of California Writers and Literature*. Issued under the auspices of the World's Fair Commission of California. San Francisco, 1893.

de Castro, Adolphe. *Portrait of Ambrose Bierce*. New York: The Century Co., 1929.

de Ford, Miriam Allen. *They Were San Franciscans*. Caldwell (Idaho): The Caxton Printers, Ltd., 1941.

De Mille, George E. *Literary Criticism in America: A Preliminary Survey*. New York: The Dial Press, Inc., 1931.

Doyle, Sir Arthur Conan. *Through the Magic Door*. Garden City: Doubleday & Company, 1919.

Falk, Robert P. "The Rise of Realism: 1871–1891." *Transitions in American Literary History*. Edited by Harry H. Clark. Durham: Duke University Press, 1953.

Fatout, Paul. *Ambrose Bierce: The Devil's Lexicographer*. Norman: University of Oklahoma Press, 1951.

Gaer, Joseph (ed.). *Ambrose Gwinett Bierce, Bibliography and Biographical Data.* California Literary Research Monograph No. 4. State Emergency Relief Administration. San Francisco, 1935.

Garland, Hamlin. *Crumbling Idols: Twelve Essays on Art Dealing Chiefly with Literature Painting and the Drama.* Edited and with an introduction by Jane Johnson. Cambridge (Massachusetts): The Belknap Press, 1960.

Grattan, C. Hartley. *Bitter Bierce: A Mystery of American Letters.* Garden City: Doubleday & Company, 1929.

Hart, James D. *The Popular Book: A History of America's Literary Taste.* New York: Oxford University Press, 1950.

Hart, Jerome A. *In Our Second Century, From an Editor's Notebook.* San Francisco: The Pioneer Press, 1931.

Hawthorne, Nathaniel. *The Complete Novels and Selected Tales of Nathaniel Hawthorne.* Edited and with an introduction by Norman Holmes Pearson. (Modern Library edition.) New York: Random House, Inc., 1937.

Hazen, General W. B. *A Narrative of Military Service.* Boston: Ticknor and Co., 1885.

Hicks, Granville. *The Great Tradition: An Interpretation of American Literature since the Civil War.* 2nd ed. revised. New York: The Macmillan Co., 1935.

Honig, Edwin. *Dark Conceit: The Making of Allegory.* Cambridge (Massachusetts): Walker-deBerry, Inc., 1960.

Howells, William Dean. *Criticism and Fiction.* New York: Harper & Row, Publishers, 1892.

Indiana at Shiloh. Report of the Commission compiled by John W. Coons. Indiana Shiloh National Park Commission, 1904.

Jordan, David Starr. *The Philosophy of Despair.* San Francisco: Paul Elder and Morgan Shepherd, 1902.

Josephson, Matthew. *Portrait of the Artist as American.* New York: Harcourt, Brace & World, Inc., 1930.

Kazin, Alfred. *On Native Grounds: An Interpretation of Modern American Prose Literature.* New York: Harcourt, Brace & World, Inc., 1942.

Knight, Grant C. *The Critical Period in American Literature.* Chapel Hill: University of North Carolina Press, 1951.

Krutch, Joseph Wood. *Edgar Allan Poe: A Study in Genius.* New York: Alfred A. Knopf, Inc., 1926.

Lewis, Oscar. *Bay Window Bohemia.* Garden City: Doubleday & Company, 1956.

Littell, Robert. "Bitter Bierce." *Read America First.* New York: Harcourt, Brace & World, Inc., 1926.

Lovecraft, Howard Phillips. *Supernatural Horror in Literature.* New York: Profile Press, 1945.

Markham, Edwin. *California the Wonderful.* New York: Hearst's International Library Co., 1910.

McCrackin, Josephine C. *The Woman Who Lost Him and Tales of the Army Frontier.* With an introduction by Ambrose Bierce. Pasadena: George Wharton James, 1913.

McWilliams, Carey. *Ambrose Bierce: A Biography.* New York: A. and C. Boni, 1929.

Mencken, H. L. "Ambrose Bierce." *Prejudices: Sixth Series.* New York: Alfred A. Knopf, Inc., 1927.

Mott, Frank Luther. *Golden Multitudes: The Story of Best Sellers in the United States.* New York: The Macmillan Co., 1947.

Mumford, Lewis. *The Golden Day: A Study in American Literature and Culture.* Boston: Beacon Press, 1957.

Murdock, Charles A. *A Backward Glance at Eighty.* San Francisco: Paul Elder and Co., 1921.

Nathan, George Jean. *The World of George Jean Nathan.* Edited by Charles Angoff. New York: Alfred A. Knopf, Inc., 1952.

Neale, Walter. *Life of Ambrose Bierce.* New York: Walter Neale, 1929.

Noel, Joseph. *Footloose in Arcadia: A Personal Record of Jack London, George Sterling, Ambrose Bierce.* New York: Carrick and Evans, 1940.

Norris, Frank. *The Responsibilities of the Novelist and Other Literary Essays.* New York: Doubleday & Company, 1903.

O'Brien, Edward J. *The Advance of the American Short Story.* Revised edition. New York: Dodd, Mead & Co., 1931.

Older, Mrs. Fremont. *William Randolph Hearst.* New York: Appleton-Century, Duell, Sloan & Pearce, 1936.

Parrington, Vernon Louis. *Main Currents in American Thought.* Vol. III: *The Beginnings of Critical Realism in America.* New York: Harcourt, Brace & World, Inc., 1930.

Parry, Albert. *Garrets and Pretenders: A History of Bohemianism in America.* New York: Corvici-Friede, 1933.

Pattee, Fred Lewis. *The Development of the American Short Story, an Historical Survey.* New York: Harper & Row, Publishers, 1923.

——. *A History of American Literature Since 1870*. New York: The Century Co., 1917.

Poe, Edgar Allan. *Selected Writings of Edgar Allan Poe*. Edited and with an introduction and notes by Edward H. Davidson. (Riverside Editions.) Boston: Houghton Mifflin Company, 1956.

Pollard, Percival. *Their Day in Court*. New York and Washington: Neale Publishing Co., 1909.

Rearden, T. H. *Petrarch and Other Essays*. With an introduction by Ambrose Bierce. San Francisco: William Doxey, 1893.

Santayana, George. *Character and Opinion in the United States*. New York: Charles Scribner's Sons, 1924.

Scarborough, Dorothy. *The Supernatural in Modern English Fiction*. New York: G. P. Putnam's Sons, 1917.

Sims, George R. *My Life: Sixty Years' Recollection of Bohemian London*. London: Eveleigh Nash Co., 1917.

Smith, Bernard. *Forces in American Criticism: A Study in the History of American Literary Thought*. New York: Harcourt, Brace & World, Inc., 1939.

Smith, Edward H. "The Ambrose Bierce Irony." *Mysteries of the Missing*. New York: The Dial Press, Inc., 1927.

Smith, Paul Jordan. "Ambrose Bierce." *On Strange Altars: A Book of Enthusiasms*. New York: A. and C. Boni, 1924.

Snell, George. *The Shapers of American Fiction: 1798–1947*. New York: E. P. Dutton & Co., Inc., 1947.

The Soldier of Indiana in the War for the Union. 2 vols. Indianapolis: Merrill and Co., 1866.

Starrett, Vincent. *Ambrose Bierce*. Chicago: Walter M. Hill, 1920.

——. *Ambrose Bierce, a Bibliography*. Philadelphia: The Centaur Book Shop, 1929.

——. "Ambrose Bierce." *Buried Caesars: Essays in Literary Appreciation*. Chicago: Corvici-McGee Co., 1923.

Sterling, George. *The Testimony of the Suns*. Including comments, suggestions, and annotations by Ambrose Bierce, together with an introduction by Oscar Lewis and a memoir of Ambrose Bierce by Albert M. Bender. San Francisco: The Book Club of California, 1927.

Stewart, Randall. *American Literature and Christian Doctrine*. Baton Rouge: Louisiana State University Press, 1958.

Walker, Franklin. *San Francisco's Literary Frontier*. New York: Alfred A. Knopf, Inc., 1939.

Ward, Alfred C. "Ambrose Bierce: 'In the Midst of Life.'" *Aspects of the Modern Short Story, English and American.* London: University of London Press, 1924.

Weeks, George F. *California Copy.* Washington: Washington College Press, 1928.

West, Ray B., Jr. *The Short Story in America: 1900–1950.* Chicago: Henry Regnery Co., 1952.

Wilson, Edmund. *Patriotic Gore: Studies in the Literature of the American Civil War.* New York: Oxford University Press, 1962.

Winn, Ralph B. *American Philosophy.* New York: Philosophical Library, Inc., 1955.

ARTICLES

"Another Attempt to Boost Bierce into Immortality," *Current Opinion,* LXV (September, 1918), 184–85.

Atherton, Gertrude. "The Literary Development of California," *Cosmopolitan,* X (January, 1891), 269–78.

Austin, Mary. "George Sterling at Carmel," *The American Mercury,* XI (May, 1927), 65–72.

———. "A Poet in Outland," *Overland Monthly,* LXXXV (November, 1927), 331, 351.

Barry, R. "The Mystery of Ambrose Bierce," *The Mentor,* IX (June, 1921), 34.

Bierce, Ambrose. "Beyond the Wall," *Cosmopolitan,* XLIV (December, 1907), 185–89.

———. "Friendship," *Cosmopolitan,* XLVI (March, 1909), 481.

———. "Small Contributions," *Cosmopolitan* XLII (March, 1907), 581–85.

———. "Small Contributions," *Cosmopolitan,* XLIV (November, 1907), 108–12.

Bierce, Helen. "Ambrose Bierce at Home," *The American Mercury,* XXX (December, 1933), 453–58.

Bower-Shore, Clifford. "Ambrose Bierce," *The Bookman* (London), LXXVIII (August, 1930), 283–84.

Boyd, E. Review of *Bitter Bierce: A Mystery of American Letters* by C. Hartley Grattan, *Outlook, CLI* (March, 1929), 470.

Braddy, Haldeen. "Ambrose Bierce and Guy de Maupassant," *American Notes and Queries,* I (August, 1941), 67–68.

——. "Trailing Ambrose Bierce," *American Notes and Queries,* I (April, May, 1941), 5–6, 20.

Budd, Louis J. "W. D. Howells' Defense of the Romance," *Publications of the Modern Language Association,* LXVII (March, 1952), 32–42.

Cann, Louise Gebhard. "Ambrose Bierce: a Rejected Guest," *The Stratford Journal,* II (June, 1918), 38–48.

Clemens, William M. "The Art of Ambrose Bierce," *The Biblio,* IV (July, 1924), 676–77.

"A Collection of Bierce Letters," *University of California Chronicle,* XXIV (January, 1932), 30–48.

Cooper, F. T. "Ambrose Bierce: an Appraisal," *Bookman,* XXXIII (July, 1911), 471–80.

de Castro, Adolphe. "Ambrose Bierce as He Really Was," *The American Parade* I (October, 1926), 28–44.

Dibble, R. F. "Ambrose Bierce," *Overland Monthly,* LXXIV (November, 1919), 418–22.

Dickson, S. B. "Ambrose Bierce, Cynical Poet and Philosopher of Old San Francisco," *Sunset Magazine,* LXIII (October, 1929), 15–16.

Dobie, Charles Caldwell. "The Man Who Short-Changed Himself," *Overland Monthly,* LXXXV (November, 1927), 327.

East, H. M., Jr. "Bierce–the Warrior Writer," *Overland Monthly,* LXV (June, 1915), 507–509.

Edwards, Herbert, "Howells and the Controversy over Realism in American Fiction," *American Literature,* III (November, 1931), 237–48.

"English Tribute to the Genius of Ambrose Bierce," *Current Opinion,* LVIII (June, 1915), 427.

Fatout, Paul. "Ambrose Bierce, Civil War Topographer," *American Literature,* XXVI (November, 1954), 391–400.

Follett, Wilson. "Ambrose Bierce, an Analysis of the Perverse Wit that Shaped His Work," *Bookman,* LXVIII (November, 1928), 284–89.

——. "Ambrose, Son of Marcus Aurelius," *Atlantic Monthly,* CLX (July, 1937), 32–42.

——. "America's Neglected Satirist," *The Dial,* LXV (July, 1918), 49–52.

——. "Bierce in His Brilliant Obscurity," *New York Times Book Review,* October 11, 1936, pp. 2, 32.

French, Joseph Lewis. "Ambrose Bierce," *Pearson's Magazine*, XXXIX (August, 1918), 245–47.

Friedrich, Otto. "The Passion of Death in Ambrose Bierce," *Zero*, II (Spring, 1956), 72–94.

Frink, Maurice M. "A Sidelight on Ambrose Bierce," *Book Notes*, I (August–September, 1923), 154.

Garnett, Porter. "Poetics, Bierce and Sterling," *Pacific Monthly*, XVIII (November, 1907), 553–58.

Goldstein, J. S. "Edwin Markham, Ambrose Bierce, and *The Man With the Hoe*," *Modern Language Notes*, LVIII (March, 1943), 165–75.

Grattan, C. Hartley. "Biography of a Journalist," *Saturday Review of Literature*, August 18, 1951, p. 11.

———. "Ambrose Bierce: Notorious Obscurian," *The Reviewer*, V (October, 1925), 103–108.

Grenander, M. E. "Bierce's Turn of the Screw: Tales of Ironical Terror," *Western Humanities Review*, XI (Summer, 1957), 257–64.

Gribble, Francis. "The Ambrose Bierce Mystery," *The Biblio*, IV (July, 1924), 673–75.

Harding, Ruth Guthrie. "Mr. Boythorn-Bierce," *Bookman*, LXI (August, 1925), 636–43.

Harte, Walter Blackburn. "A Tribute to Ambrose Bierce," *The Biblio*, IV (July, 1924), 680–81.

Havighurst, W. "He Never Stopped Swinging," *Saturday Review of Literature*, January 25, 1947, p. 16.

Hubbard, Elbert. Review of *The Collected Works*, Vol. I, *The Fra*, III (May, 1909), 29–31.

Jeffers, Robinson. "A Few Memories," *Overland Monthly*, LXXXV (November, 1927), 329, 351.

Jones, Idwal. "San Francisco: an Elegy," *The American Mercury*, V (August, 1925), 477–84.

Kenton, Edna. "Ambrose Bierce and 'Moxon's Master,'" *Bookman*, LXII (September, 1925), 71–79.

Klein, Marcus. "San Francisco and Her Hateful Ambrose Bierce," *Hudson Review*, VII (Autumn, 1954), 392–407.

Lal, Golind Behari. "George Sterling's Bohemian Creed," *Overland Monthly*, LXXXV (December, 1927), 369.

Lambert, Mary. "A Trio of California Poets," *Pacific Town Talk*, December 18, 1897, pp. 26–27.

Leary, Lewis. "Bierce in Business," *Saturday Review of Literature*, June 9, 1956, p. 20.

Leof, Madelin. "On Genuine Wit," *Literary Review*, IV (July, 1924), 902.

Lewis, Austin. "George Sterling at Play," *Overland Monthly*, LXXXV (November, 1927), 344.

Littell, Robert. "Bitter Bierce," *The New Republic*, XL (October, 1924), 177.

London, Charmian Kittredge. "George Sterling as I Knew Him," *Overland Monthly*, LXXXV (March, 1927), 69–70, 76, 80, 83, 87, 90–91.

Lovett, R. M. "Five Books on Ambrose Bierce," *American Literature*, I (January, 1930), 434–39.

McCrackin, Mrs. Josephine C. "Reminiscences of Bret Harte and Pioneer Days in the West," *Overland Monthly*, LXVII (January, 1916), 7–15.

McWilliams, Carey. "Ambrose Bierce," *The American Mercury*, XVI (February, 1929), 215–22.

———. "Ambrose Bierce and His First Love," *Bookman*, LXXV (June, 1932), 254–59.

———. "The Mystery of Ambrose Bierce," *The American Mercury*, XXII (March, 1931), 330–37.

———. "Roosevelt Johnson Becomes Reminiscent," *Overland Monthly*, LXXXV (December, 1927), 367.

Mencken, H. L. "Ambrose Bierce Mystery," *The American Mercury* XVIII (September, 1929), 124–26.

Millard Bailey. "The Launching of a Famous Poem," *Bookman*, XXVII (May, 1908), 267–72.

———. "Personal Memories of Ambrose Bierce," *Bookman*, XL (February, 1915), 653–58.

Miller, Arthur E. "The Influence of Edgar Allan Poe on Ambrose Bierce," *American Literature*, IV (May, 1932), 130–50.

"Mr. Bierce's War Club," *Bookman*, XXX (October, 1909), 124–25.

Monaghan, Frank. "Ambrose Bierce and the Authorship of *The Monk and the Hangman's Daughter*," *American Literature*, II (January, 1931), 337–49.

Monahan, Michael. "Our Greatest Poet," *The Papyrus*, I (October, 1907), 1–8.

Nathan, George Jean. "Ambrose Light," *The American Mercury*, II (February, 1934), 2.

Nations, Leroy J. "Ambrose Bierce: the Gray Wolf of American Letters," *South Atlantic Quarterly*, XXV (July, 1926), 253–68.

"New Letters of Ambrose Bierce," *Opinion*, II (May, 1930), 3–4.

O'Day, Edward F. "1869-1926," *Overland Monthly*, LXXXV (December, 1927), 357–58, 383.

Oehser, P. H. "Ambrose Bierce's Centenary," *Saturday Review of Literature*, November 21, 1942, p. 11.

Partridge, Eric. "Ambrose Bierce," *The London Mercury*, XVI (October, 1927), 625–38.

Poore, E. G. "Ambrose Bierce's Last Tilt with Mars," *New York Times Magazine*, January 1, 1928.

"Prophetic Powers of Bierce," *Bookman*, XXX (October, 1909), 120–22.

Prussia, George. "Ambrose Bierce," *The Wave*, September 22, 1894, p. 13.

Review of *Can Such Things Be?*, *The Nation*, CVII (November, 1918), 628.

Review of *In the Midst of Life*, *The Atheneum*, February 20, 1892, p. 241.

Review of *In the Midst of Life*, *The Nation*, LXVI (March, 1898), 225.

Review of *In the Midst of Life*, *The Nation*, CVII (August, 1918), 232.

Review of *The Collected Works*, Vol. I, *The Atheneum*, July 3, 1909, p. 8.

Review of *The Collected Works*, Vol. II, *The Atheneum*, March 26, 1910, p. 367.

Review of *The Collected Works*, Vol. III, *The Atheneum*, June 11, 1910, p. 702.

Review of *The Collected Works*, Vols. VII–X, *The Atheneum*, September 16, 1911, pp. 322–23.

Rideing, William H. "A Corner of Bohemia," *Bookman*, XXXII (February, 1911), 620–29.

Rorty, James. "Living Inseparables," *Overland Monthly*, LXXXV (December, 1927), 366.

Scheffauer, Herman. "The Death of Satire," *The Living Age*, CCLXXVIII (July, 1913), 82–90.

———. "The Satirist in Vacuo," *Freeman*, I (August, 1920), 514–16.

Sinclair, Upton. "My Friend, George Sterling," *Overland Monthly*, LXXXV (November, 1927), 365.

Smith, H. Greenbough. "Bierce's Devil Dictionary," *The Biblio*, IV (July, 1924), 678–80.

Snell, George. "Poe Redivivius," *Arizona Quarterly*, I (Summer, 1945), 49–57.

Sterling, George. "The Shadow Maker," *The American Mercury*, VI (September, 1925), 10–19.

———. "A Wine of Wizardry," *Cosmopolitan*, XLIII (September, 1909), 551–56.

"Two Essayists," *The Nation*, XXCIX (September, 1909), 306–307.

"The Underground Reputation of Ambrose Bierce," *Current Literature*, XLVII (September, 1909), 279–81.

West, George. "The California Literati," *The American Mercury*, VIII (July, 1926), 281–86.

Williams, S. T. "Ambrose Bierce and Bret Harte," *American Literature*, XVII (May, 1945), 179–80.

Wilson, Edmund. "Ambrose Bierce on the Owl Creek Bridge," *The New Yorker*, December 8, 1951, pp. 60 ff.

Wilt, Napier. "Ambrose Bierce and the Civil War," *American Literature*, I (November, 1929), 260–85.

UNPUBLISHED MATERIAL

Bierce, Ambrose. Twenty-three letters to Charles Warren Stoddard.

Emmons, Winfred S. "The Materials and Methods of American Horror Fiction in the Nineteenth Century." Unpublished Ph.D. dissertation, Louisiana State University, 1952.

Flinn, Eugene C. "Ambrose Bierce and the Journalization of the American Short Story." Unpublished Ph.D. dissertation, St. John's (Brooklyn), 1954.

Grenander, Mary E. "The Critical Theories of Ambrose Bierce." Unpublished Ph.D. dissertation, University of Chicago, 1949.

Smith, Rebecca W. "The Civil War and Its Aftermath in American Fiction, 1861–1899, with a Dictionary Catalogue and Indexes." Unpublished Ph.D. dissertation, University of Chicago, 1932.

Index of Titles